PERSIAN BROCADE, LATE SIXTEENTH CENTURY

WEAVES AND DRAPERIES

WEAVES AND DRAPERIES

Classic and Modern

BY

HELEN CHURCHILL CANDEE

AUTHOR OF "THE TAPESTRY BOOK," "DECORATIVE STYLES
AND PERIODS," ETC.

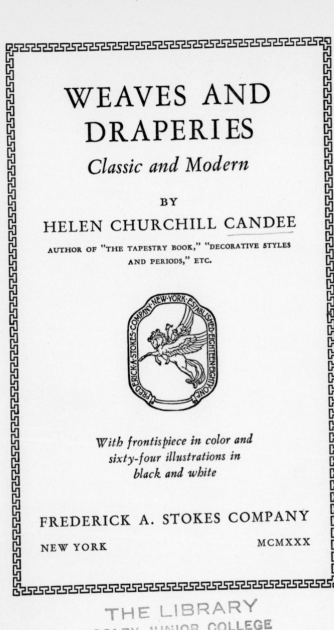

*With frontispiece in color and
sixty-four illustrations in
black and white*

FREDERICK A. STOKES COMPANY

NEW YORK   MCMXXX

Printed in the United States of America

To

ELLEN ENNIS

A Booklover

whose keen discrimination and apt counsel
inspire those who write and those who read

Acknowledgment is here made to the photograph department of the Metropolitan Museum for the majority of illustrations, and gratitude is offered to Miss Frances Morris, curator of textiles.

CONTENTS

LIST OF ILLUSTRATIONS

xi

ILLUSTRATIONS

ILLUSTRATIONS

ILLUSTRATIONS

xiv

ILLUSTRATIONS

XV

ILLUSTRATIONS

WEAVES AND DRAPERIES

CHAPTER I

ORIGINALS AND COPIES

WHEREVER hangs a drapery, there hangs a tale.
But it is not even considered until one cares
enough about the mute thing to examine into its past,
into the reasons why it is of that particular weave, color
and design.

And not knowing these things, the assemblage of
draperies needed to soften the aspect of our rooms
sometimes fails in taste and in that intelligent selection
which produces harmony. Decorative textiles plead
for proper associates, but their language is not audible.
The velvets of Genoa in the Fourteenth Century beg to
be relieved from their place as coverlet to a Louis XVI
chaise-longue; the fabrics of modernist art shriek a protest when displayed amid Grinling Gibbons' wood
carvings; and these cries should be understood.

It is to prevent such ill-planned mating that this
book is offered. By their stories are the textiles known,
and by these same tales do we know instinctively where

I

and how to place them. The stories are so numerous as to suggest the thousand and one tales of Scheherazade, but we will shorten them to a more convenient length to suit the times. Like those famous stories of beguilement they carry us first into the East, for weaving is a prehistoric art, and the cradle of mankind who invented it was rocked in the valley of the Euphrates or thereabouts. Had that same *menschenkind* been willing to limit his living to hot countries, possibly weaving would have had no reason for supplanting fig-leaves as dress and palms as upholstery. But man was, and is, prone to wander, and wandering he shivered, and so came woven cloth.

The tale of looms leads back to the time of shadows; maybe it suggests unpleasant things like cave-dwellers and the Neanderthal Man, so for pride's and comfort's sake let those who are interested start with the loom of Penelope's web and those other more productive looms of her time, for here we have old Greek vases to instruct us with their drawings.

Books and books are written upon looms, and these explain with scientific care the machinery that has grown so complicated. But it is not necessary to know

2

COPTIC ORNAMENT IN TAPESTRY TECHNIQUE, WOOL ON
A GARMENT OF COTTON.   FOURTH CENTURY WHEN
ROMAN EMPIRE DOMINATED EGYPT IN POLITICS AND
IN ART

COPTIC DRESS ORNAMENT, TAPESTRY WEAVE, THIRD
OR FOURTH CENTURY

them, or to accomplish the understanding of every play of warp and weft—or woof, if you like that word better. That we leave in the hands of the weaver. But it is of interest to us to know that all looms were operated by hand until the Eighteenth Century, a process so slow and painful that the wonder ever grows how the weavers could supply the enormous amount of fabrics demanded by the increase in luxury after the Middle Ages.

The great fact of interest is that when the weaving became most complicated one there was who came to the fore with a gift to the world in his hand. It was Joseph Marie Jacquard, who in 1801 to 1804 perfected the wonderful loom which produced complicated patterns by means of perforated cards. Three other men had contributed their share to this invention, Bouchon, Falcon, Vaucanson.

It happened about 1801 that a certain loom belonging to the State was seriously out of repair. Jacquard, who was known as an able mechanician, was called to make it operative. While at work he applied improvements of his own invention and of others', and the resulting loom was called after him. It did not spring at once

3

into perfection, but was the effect of combining inventions which had appeared throughout preceding years. At about this time the power loom was taking the place of the hand loom.

Fortunately it is not necessary for our use of textiles to know how the shuttle which carries the weft is thrown, nor how the warp threads are separated, nor how two weaves are carried on at the same time on two warps, the two fabrics commingling at the dictates of the pattern.

It is enough that we know the names and aspects of the materials oftenest in hand, the primary ones of which are tapestry, taffeta, sarcenet, satin, velvet, damask, brocade. And practically every one knows those; every woman is forced to or she cannot go a-shopping, and every man knows them because of his interest in woman. He may not in these days—more's the pity— wear satin knee breeches with coat of rich brocade, but he finds his thrill is watching his lady, satin-clad, reclining on rich damask—and thus he learns his textile lesson and develops fondness for the fabrics.

We of the beauty-loving eye are ready to pass quickly over the mechanical processes that we may reach the completed product. It is there we find the diversion of romance. The completed fabric alone shows us the design, the ornament, and in that ornament lies all the history of the alluring East, of Europe and even of our new America.

Our chief pleasure will be in reviewing the ornament, for that way lies romance and history. There also lies our way to a logical taste in using the materials in hand, for they all speak of the time and place of their origin.

The reason for designs, too, is a part of the pleasure hidden in them. Why do the early Persian silks bear figures of horsemen shooting at deer or at lions, as their horses gallop madly? Why are Spanish fabrics haunted with suggestions of the Orient? Why have French textiles of the Eighteenth Century so strong a taste of an exotic Chinese element?

All ornament is symbol, and what is symbol but a compressed tablet of history or experience? This means that a story lies in each design; it may be the story of a religion, as in arabesques; or of a beautiful superstition, as the tree-of-life; or of history, as in Napoleon's bee. To discover these symbols in our sur-

5

roundings is to enrich the life of everyday. I know no greater pleasure than a moment spent in intimacy with the textiles of one's own apartments if one possess the key to the origin of each. When once the eyes are opened to what they mean, designs are living evidence of a vital past, and must often seize a delighted attention.

That we cannot clothe our persons nor dress our houses and theaters in textiles woven in the time of their first production, drives us to reproductions of the old designs, but that need trouble us not at all. The most thrilling in design of all textiles, the Coptic wools, the Sassanian and Sicilian silks—what remains of them but tired bits resting in museums? And the glowing velvets that crept from the Mohammedan Empire into awakened Italy, and the fabrics of Italy's Renaissance? If we have them it is solely as bibelots.

Only in their recent copies are they of real service as coverings and hangings. The small lengths that Time has allowed to pass his destroying fingers are venerable aristocrats which we adore but from which we expect no service. We line them to spare their weak fabric, we edge them with a protecting galloon

6

and place them about on tables or walls as an evidence of a cultivated taste in luxuries, and for the esthetic thrills received in studying them. Therefore we bless the able silk mills of today which keep alive for us the old ornament so full of beauty and tradition. These mills all have their private museums of old textiles, and are constantly acquiring old bits over which an expert pores as over a volume of ancient lore, picking and plucking at threads to divine the secrets of the weave, and setting artists to work to copy the design in the technique of the weaver.

Just one thing is allowed to mar the beauty of the copy—the effort to cheapen the cost of the reproduction. If a new-made fabric loses beauty by reason of a design mal-copied or a double weft avoided, it is that the manufacturer may save that way. But in-so-far as the old model is carefully followed, the old symbolism preserved, the result is fit for our fastidious use.

The Eighteenth Century has left us much of its damask and velvet which were used as hangings in cathedrals. Shrewd buyers of antique stuffs for the great market of America made the discovery that the lesser among the clergy and the greater among the servitors could be won into giving up the old and disused silks of churches hard-pressed for money. It is these which provided wall hangings for many a collector's home. But now even these have been absorbed and it is doubtful if in these days any one is offered a hanging of one or two hundred yards of rich rose velvet or red damask.

But here again is a little knowledge of old textiles useful, for equipped with that one can choose from among the new a weave that bears some of the charm imparted by the older weavers. In damask it is found in purity of design and beauty of color. In velvets it is found in the pile, when it is deep and delicately irregular as in the Sixteenth Century and not close and short as in our own time. *Apropos des bottes,* as the French expression says, old fabrics of Europe are always narrow, the double width being unknown on the handloom.

This is the reason for not insisting on the antique fabrics: that they are almost impossible to obtain; and this is the reason for upholding new manufacture: that the looms are giving out textiles which satisfy a cultivated taste and which enable us to renew the draperies of the period room—the room *en style*—when time has caused the original ones to perish.

The fashion in draperies follows the fashion of dress, a woman's dress, in recent centuries. It is an amusing thought; follow it out and see how human it makes the window and furniture draperies of the recognized periods and styles of decoration. In the times of "the Louis'" when women's dresses were bouffant, were looped in festoons, trimmed with yards and yards of frills and fringes, were not windows, couches and beds similarly shaded with voluminous folds and garnitures? And when Napoleonic styles succeeded, did not a sort of self-conscious moral rectitude express itself in straight lines and lessened yardage for both women and windows?

And there are our own amazing times, when much that is superfluous is eliminated. Curtains and frocks not only hang straight and clear the floor, but the old-time underfurnishings are left off—in both cases. Time was when a taffeta curtain was lined and interlined with canton flannel, with cotton cloth, with Shantung silk, for layer upon layer was the upholsterer's delight.

9

Time was, too, when the flannel petticoat was as much a part of a lady's person as her fingernails.

As for beds, they not only took upon themselves all suggestions that skirts had to offer, but they actually added hats! Look at the tufts of ostrich plumes nodding from the canopy of a monarch's bed in Louis XV's time. Now that our hats go untrimmed, the bedpost thrusts its pineapple top freely into the purer air, or there are no posts at all.

And so it goes, woman's fancy in dress is reflected in her surroundings. This may come from man's desire to please the capricious creature, for men are, after all, the most creative of the decorators. It has always been, it will always be, that decorations are primarily composed for women. And as men invent the great styles, it is not too much to say that they can be looked on as a gift of devotion, an act of homage. We speak now of the time since Louis XIV. The Sun King was too obsessed with his own importance to think of furnishings beyond his own, which were a glorification of his exalted position in the world. Fancying himself at times a reincarnation of the Roman emperor, Alexander the Great, the ornament

COPTIC, SIXTH OR SEVENTH CENTURY, WOVEN IN SILK, REPRE-
SENTING A HUNT ENCLOSED IN A CIRCLE. THE SAME DESIGN
APPEARS IN PERSIA, FIFTH CENTURY

SYRIAN OR COPTIC SERGE SILK OF SEVENTH CENTURY,
TREE OF LIFE ENCLOSED IN CIRCLE

of his time took on the flavor of conquest, and of a magnificent government.

Not much in this was feminine. Important women of the time were bound to be serious and intellectual; they studied philosophy under Montaigne and Saint Evremond, and wit under Molière, and formed salons like that of Madame de Rambouillet, where intellects met and virtue was magnified.

But in the next reign the monarch and his State management were less conspicuous than when Louis the Great ruled. The women of the time were glorified, and their tastes were exploited. La Pompadour and Du Barry were the inspiration, and from their time on the decorator has kept woman in mind when practising his art.

Even the new type of woman that our own time has produced is very evidently the inspiration for the new-art decorations and the odd fabrics it employs.

CHAPTER II

THE technique of weaving is so varied and complicated a matter that it can only be described with
the loom before the demonstrator, but the woven fabric
is a matter with which we should be familiar in all its
expressions. Perhaps then a few definitions may not
make too dull a reading.

The primary weave of "one over, one under," is
exemplified in most textiles of even surface. The tapestry weave, being the next, when considered chronologically, is a variant of that, with the weft threads
thrown only the length of a detail of the pattern instead of away across the loom. Incidentally this last
must be hand work or it fails in esthetic value. Serge
or diagonal is made by passing the woof thread over
two and under one, or similar irregularities. Satin has
a surface almost entirely of warp thread. Damask
(named from Damascus) is woven from a pattern, this
design being represented by the interplay of two
weaves. The reverse side also carries the pattern but
reverses the weave. Brocade is far more elaborate, for

12

it may combine an infinite variety of colors, and of weave, besides introducing metal threads. Brocade is a weave in which the extra threads that make the design are employed only for the design and are not thrown from selvedge to selvedge except as a float seen only on the reverse between the figures. Respect for the weaver increases to amazement if one examines the threads of the brocades in the centuries before Jacquard invented his loom. Every weave went into these old brocades, even velvet, and threads of gold and silver of two kinds were introduced in the same pattern. Pick up at random a piece of brocaded silk of the Eighteenth Century and examine the scattered bouquets of flowers thrown on its background of elaborate weave. To heighten the effect the design is liberally dashed with gold or silver of a thread compounded of silk and metal twisted, and of a thread which is a fine strip of the metal alone. And such is the quality of the metal that time has had no effect upon it, and it glows against the background of salmon pink or turquoise deliciously clouded with fading.

Brocatelle we class among the damasks, but so much of linen or cotton often goes into its composition that it takes on a heavy richness all its own, dependent upon mass. It is thick, stiff, elegant, and in its olden colors is a delight. Lampas is its near relation. These weaves are made now but are softer and mellower in the antique fabric than in the new.

Cloth of gold and velvet each has its history. The most alluring fabric in the world of decoration is velvet. It has magic in its folds, for it makes all things animate and inanimate look better than they really are. It is the ideal background for emphasizing beauty. Even portraits of mediocre quality are glorified into works of art by being hung against a square of rich old velvet.

The mystery of the weaving of the alluring fabric is a part of its charm. For long I refused to learn how it was made, preferring to accept it as an unknown process entirely in the hands of unseen gods who drift around looms and direct their production. A flower full of sentiment is a thing one can never bear to tear apart in the interests of botany. All this being mere folly, we will forget that velvet has strange and winning qualities, peculiarly its own, and will turn to its origins. Of course they entice us again into the East, that being the region of beginnings.

14

BROCADE WOVEN IN SPAIN IN THE EIGHTEENTH CEN-
TURY, BUT REPEATING SARACENIC MOTIVES DERIVED
FROM SASSANIAN, USED IN SICILY IN THE TWELFTH
CENTURY. ANIMALS ENCLOSED IN LARGE ROUNDELS,
CONNECTED WITH SMALLER ONES WERE A FEATURE
OF PERSIAN OR SASSANIAN DESIGNS FROM THE SIXTH
TO THE FOURTEENTH CENTURIES

SICILIAN SILK, BUFF AND GREEN WITH THREADS
OF SILVER. THE ORIENTAL PAIRED ANIMALS ARE
NO LONGER ENCLOSED IN A ROUNDEL

There is a suspicion that the fabric was invented as a refinement of the weave of the rug in Persia. But the manner of making requires an entirely different technique. Whereas the pile of a rug is tied in, knot by knot, twisted around underlying threads, velvet is woven on a loom. It is of two warps, one over the other, the upper one being looped on wires which are withdrawn and the surface is cut to form the pile.

It is a sort of weaver's magic, yet velvet is one of the most usual weaves and is accepted without a thrill, or a thought for those long-ago people who so patiently worked out a process. Ungrateful are we of the present time, ungrateful for our heritage of beautiful crafts.

The weaves of ancient velvet are many. The plain is called cut velvet, the brocaded is called voided, the looped is called uncut, and ciselé or chiseled is a combination of both. A most enchanting process is the pile-on-pile, which was produced with long and short loops made with small and large wire, which gave two or even three thicknesses for the design to enjoy. But, alas, it is only in collections that examples can be seen of the rich beauty of its profound shadows and gleaming color. It was made in the leisure of the times we miscall Gothic. Stamped velvet is made by impressing the pattern with hot irons, printed velvet by stamping in color after the manner of printing less elegant fabrics.

We are on datable ground no earlier than the Fourteenth Century, and that in Italy, from whence came Europe's greatest supply through the Fifteenth and Sixteenth Centuries. Persia wove the most exquisite velvets of Asia during the reign of Shah Abbas (1586-1644) and just before.

As the fabric was made with two warps, the foundation weave could be treated separately; that is, it could be woven in satin, or plain silk, or, more intricate still, it could be brocaded. Uncut loops were a later development.

Thus the weavers had in their hands the possibility of endless variety, and thence came the barbarically magnificent velvets of the late Gothic and early Renaissance to astound the world of Europe. It is to Europe that velvets especially belong because of their lavish use in that part of the world. That perhaps may have been a matter of climate. Where the winter winds blow cold, there is a natural longing on the part of man to dress his person and line his habitat with textiles suggesting warmth.

One of the earliest among the combinations of background and pile is the Gothic velvet which has a design of the Florentine artichoke and its enclosing circle merely traced, scarcely interrupting the smooth flow of plain velvet. There is another straying design which bears the technical foreign name of *ferronnière,* which suggests the pattern being traced in wrought iron. But a few years ago the dealers in Florence were offering it in squares of a meter and a half; but now—now one stands and admires in museums and private collections. "You may look but you may not touch," as is said to little boys in the cake-shop.

Big designs soon followed. The background became more elaborate and there came the fashion of the heavy diagonal stem bearing pomegranates, or artichokes, in such variety of conventionalization as makes differentiation a study for the specialist.

Gold came early into favor to combine with velvet, and gave the name of cloth of gold to the fabric. Sometimes the background was a glittering field of gold on which was thrown a bold design, or again the velvet covered almost all the surface with the ornament wrought in gold. If very little of these stuffs for regal pageantry remains today, it may be because at the decay of the textile the gold was extracted by firing, to use in other ways. Many a purse of the nobility depleted by wars has been filled this way.

At the earliest time, when velvet was being woven in the north of Italy, the Ottoman Empire to the East of them was in close touch through the markets of Constantinople and the trade of Venice, and Genoa. Turkish velvets contemporary with those of Europe resemble them, although the design is bolder, never reaching the intellectual quality of awakened Europe. The masterful display of the Turk, his desire for show, for the evidences of dominance, are plainly read in the designs of his velvets and brocades. And yet, they can sometimes be confused with the Italian.

Let us not decry the perfection of the looms of today, for they copy with fidelity the old velvets. Hand-looms are in use in Italy for velvets which need the slight imperfections or variations of the individual to give them character. With a love which begets devotion the weavers work to preserve the old models and ideals and even factories give us velvets, specially plain ones, which imitate well the deep heavy pile of the Fifteenth Century.

When the Renaissance declined, its first textile evidence was the lack of thought in design. Show took the place of thought, and patterns expanded into areas of complicated drawing. But a little later, especially when cut and uncut were used together, came a fresh inspiration, a revolt against size, a sudden fashion for small design, like sprigs, sown all over a background usually of satin. This was in the Seventeenth Century.

In the time of Louis XIV no less an artist than Daniel Marot gave himself to the drawing of designs for velvet brocades. It will be remembered that he was the architect called to England to enlarge the palace of Hampton Court. When we think on the men of talent who created the textile designs from the Fifteenth through the Eighteenth Centuries the wonder ceases that they continue to be copied.

THE WEAVERS

Through all the romance of weaving and design runs the tale of the weavers. They are not always in the lime-light, these busy people of a half submerged class, but at times come to the front of the stage and endow their work with an interest deeply human.

To go back to very early textiles, there were the able Coptic weavers who were producing exquisite work in tapestry stitch from the beginning of our era, all through the Roman Empire and into the Mohammedan domination. They were weaving when the Romans came and took possession of their land and their freedom. The conquerors, not slow to appreciate the value of their work, attached them as part of the plunder, and thus the Coptic weavers were made slaves—not slaves under the lash, merely owned, so that their work might belong to the master. Increase in production, yes, for the new invaders wanted cloths and clothing, but it must be that they were happy, to produce such joyous works as some of the Coptic weavings in wool—and yes, also in silk, that rarest material which ships and camels brought sparingly from immeasurable distance.

The weavers of Sicily—drawn from India, Persia and Byzantium—came to the fore in the Mohammedan dominance, and grew to such fame that they were coaxed away after Moorish power faded and Italian power arose. It was Lucca who drew them to herself in the Thirteenth Century, when silk culture was established in Italy, and Lucca was not only a city but a State, including all the country around. That made of the weavers adventurers and travelers, and, plucking them from the arabesques and interlacing of Mohammedan thought, threw them into the wealth of design flowing from the Far East and then being developed through Gothic and Byzantine art into the Renaissance.

Thus it has ever been, large bodies of able weavers, removed from their native land, effecting a tremendous change in the centers of textile production. Lucca had the famed Sicilian weavers but a short time, however, for in 1315, only fifty years after their coming, they were enticed away by the Florentines. It was probably with gay step that they went, for all the world of artists and intellectuals turned to Florence, the first city of the great awakening. The designs then were going through transitions and attaining the general character we miscall Gothic. How came the word? Not from intention to designate the Goths who long ago had ceased invasions and had been absorbed, but to describe the Germans and the French and others of the North who had evolved the style of the great cathedrals.

The history of Flanders is deeply concerned with weavers, especially the weavers of wool. That little country has ever been a morsel desired of kings. Its ownership or control figures in war after war. Especially did the wars of religion affect its weaving population. All through the second half of the Sixteenth Century Europe was the battle-ground of Protestant and Catholic. Burnings and massacres took place whenever religious zeal or political ambition was gratified thereby. The famous Edict of Nantes was issued by France's great king, Henry IV (of Navarre). He being born a Protestant, yet called to rule over France, followed the way of least resistance and declared himself a Catholic. But in the hope of lessening the sickening conflict he published in 1598 the Edict, which gave Protestants the right to worship in their own manner undisturbed, but before that many weavers had fled, some to Kent in England.

It was Louis XIV who in 1685 revoked the Edict,

and then came a rush of the Protestant weavers to Flanders. Many looms being in the north of France, and guilds of weavers being existent in Flanders it was natural to turn for safety to this sure and sympathetic country. The effect on Flanders was to increase her trade and her production but by this means France lost her ablest weavers. This was the time, we remember, when Louis XIV was using the best artists and weavers in France at the Royal Factory of the Gobelins and in Lyons. Those he lost to Flanders, and to England, to the enrichment of those countries.

England under the Tudors was busy with looms. The nation's rulers saw the prosperity of the country in the hands of the weaver. Incredible. Yet it illustrates the importance of the man at the loom.

Elizabeth founded on this industry the commerce of the nation, building on an ingenious scheme. Her merchant marine was seriously inaugurated that she might have her own carriers from the ports of the Mediterranean and further East, and that she might send her ships out loaded with English cloth.

Captains of vessels had strict orders to dispose of these cargoes in wholesale if possible, but if necessary to force a piece at a time on the foreign merchants for their own personal use. Woolen hangings and drapings, woolen covers for beds and cushions then became the mode in Europe for those who found silk too dear. The raising of sheep grew apace for their fleecy wool, and dyes were sought. Asiatic dyes were unquestionably good, but with financial prudence Elizabeth set her people to find them at less cost. So it came that the forests and valleys of Virginia were scientifically searched for vegetation or minerals of durable and pleasing color. In Cromwell's time England's textile industry required a cloth fleet, and of broadcloth alone twenty thousand bales a year were exported by means of these vessels.

Lyons came early to the fore as a center for the weaving of silks. We hear of weavers there as early as 1450 under Charles VII, and of many more under the wise direction of Henri IV. Under the latter the looms grew to twelve thousand. The revocation of the Edict of Nantes reduced this number to three thousand. The coming of those weavers to England, flying before persecution, caused the establishment of the Spitalfields looms, which are even to-day the center of Britain's silk industry. Lyons today has over three hundred thousand weavers and dyers and other textile workers. After the French Revolution they again began to gather there, and when Jacquard's loom was invented shortly after 1800 the number greatly increased. This loom lightened labor, but increased the amount of production, so more weavers were required.

ORNAMENT IN OLD TEXTILES

In the search for the origin of textile design or ornament, a delightful element of adventure appears when the line carries back to the Year One and, disregarding that barrier, crashes through into the B.C. dates. To understand the motives which we are even now reproducing, we must catch a glimpse of the youthful Cyrus (he lived but thirty-one years) as he pushed eastwards in the interests of Greece and founded the Persian Empire in B.C. 226, taking Babylon on the way.

It was the second dynasty after Cyrus that was called Sassanian, which lasted until A.D. 637, and is of special interest because we are even now using the ornament composed by those early Persians. It was they who impressed upon the world of design the simple expedient of a large roundel enclosing a single figure or a scene. The roundel was delicately ornamented within its clean-cut band, earlier with small discs, later with flat rose petals, and later still with scrolls. Within the circle was a single wild beast or one entirely fabulous until the fashion came of setting two beasts within the roundel, back to back or confronted. Later still came birds, not the lovely bulbul of the Persian poets, but the aggressive parrot, with his air of resentment and his suggestive beak.

The charm of the oldest textile ornament is found in flatness of pattern and the absence of modeling.

Within the circle of one of the most delightful of the old designs is a pair of lithe young kings vigorously hunting a pair of lions. The lions crouch for a spring, the horses leap with excitement, the agile kings discharge the arrow from the bow, and all this is arranged with a balance as perfect as though a geometric touch had ordered it. More than appears is implied by the roundel. It is intended to enclose a forest and to exclude any habitation. The forested mountains of Persia were full of wild beasts. A man was not a man unless he went in pursuit of them, and a king must show himself in all things the superior of other men. Thus we have a glimpse of the life of people who have sent the pictured roundels rolling down the centuries to our own time, when the looms of Italy are copying them. Amusingly enough, they pass as a novelty to the uninformed, but even so arrest attention and inspire delight. By some good fortune a few of these Sassanian textiles have been preserved, some of them having been laid away in tombs of celebrated bishops, and recently put in museums.

The picturesque touch of the traders is a part of Sassanian study. Through Persia lay one of the great trade routes connecting China and also India with the West. The designs of these two countries affected the Sassanians when they were thus brought into their country. The packs of the camel-trains from the artistic East were opened along the journey, sometimes bought entire by the Persian merchants, so found their journey's end among the people of the Sassanian dynasty. These same camels were loaded with new goods and continued westward taking their special Persian textiles to Babylon, Damascus, and so on to Byzantium, which was then struggling to maintain itself as a capital of the disintegrating Roman Empire.

But the deposit of figured textiles left in Persia by the camel-train of the trade route, bore strange designs which afterward crept into the Sassanian drawings. The roundel itself was one of the motives of the Chinese and bore as its earliest ornament the little discs that followed each other around the circle. To the swastika, or fylfot, China has ever been faithful, even to the present day, but as this ornament is one of those found in the early art of all races, it cannot belong solely to one. Chinese cloud motives, however, appeared in Persia but with curious local alteration. Sassanian weaves are not without a trace of the Hellenistic culture. These turn us at once back to the remote time when Alexander the Great, the amazingly young conqueror, sowed the seeds of Greek art throughout the entire East. The floriated scroll of Greece and Rome appeared in China, India, Persia; the palmette and honeysuckle gave to other peoples an idea which they developed with local vegetation.

Byzantium flavored by Rome was rich in these and other Hellenistic motives, but at about the Sixth Century, when Rome had declined and Persia was active with a brilliant civilization, there came an intermingling of the two countries in the matter of design. The church of St. Sophia was dedicated at this time, and Ravenna fell before the men of Constantinople—Byzantium. The Roman art stiffened under new influences, grew conventional, lost its free movements and crystallized into the formality we know as Byzantine. But Persia's contribution lay in the way of ornament for weaving, and thus we have a confusion or rather a similarity between woven designs of the Sassanian kings and those of the Byzantines. The stiff pairs of birds or animals which are back to back or confronted are distinctly a Sassanian contribution, and are apt to confuse the enthusiast who seeks for origins. The Persian or Sassanian animals have a movement and vitality suggesting life, whereas those drawn under Byzantine influence are stiff and heraldic, emblems rather than pictures. Later they became freed from their enclosing roundel.

Constantinople, to use its modern name, became a Moslem city in the time of the Mohammedan conquests. It became the pearl for which two dragons were ever contesting, Asia to the East and Europe to the West. Moreover, it was the gateway to trade, and that led to Venice and her woven designs—but that came in the Renaissance.

From India came the elephant, sometimes coupled with the tree-of-life, which is Persian, and these are woven into silks of Byzantium, some of which are still extant. But this ancient elephant has amusing qualities and outlines all his own; his legs are long and slender, his toes are sharp, his trunk is many-jointed. And the tree-of-life beside him is a symmetry of Persian ornament in vegetation. How little the gay summer crowd at fashionable Le Touquet could divine that such elephants, silk-woven, were hid in the near-by church resting obscurely in the inactive village of St. Josse. Such a textile was found in a hidden recess behind the altar but a decade ago, and carried with the antiquarian's joy to repose in a silk museum at Lyons. Through such happenings as this we touch the patterns of the early weavers.

Indian civilization is so old that the young Alexander the Great found it in an advanced state when in his thirst for conquest he reached it in 327 B.C. We owe to it much that has been ignored by a limited Euro-

SPANISH OR SICILIAN DAMASK OF THE FOURTEENTH
CENTURY.   PAIRED ANIMALS ARE HERE USED BUT
ARE NO LONGER SHUT WITHIN A FRAME, ROUND OR
OGIVAL

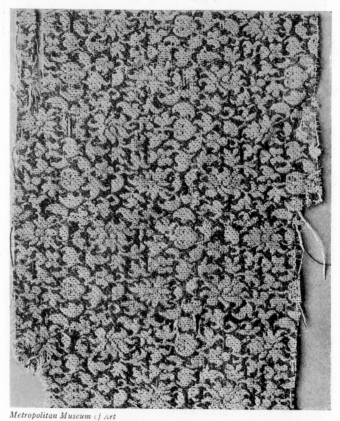

CHINESE TEXTILE INTERRED WITH POPE BENEDICT XI
IN 1304, IN GOLD AND WHITE, THE GOLD THREADS
MADE OF STRIPS OF GOLD LEAF PASTED ON TOUGH
PAPER OR CATGUT

pean view. Weaving and design in India kept pace with Persia; indeed the two are equally advanced and equally prolific throughout the ages. The materials used for fine textiles were wool of camels and cotton, and more sparsely, silk. Gold came ever into lavish use considering its value. The Indian pine is the figure most familiar, for although almost prehistoric it still persists and is known to all. In the Ghandaran period of Indian art, Hellenistic motives prevailed, and in the pictured caves of Ajanta, we find the clue to the most beautiful of Indian ornament—all of which had its effect on Indian weaving.

China, holding in its hand the most perfect thread for weaving in all the world, and having an art of high development many centuries before the Christian era, has the history of weaving united with the history of silk, and in that it is best examined.

The Moslem domination occurred in the Seventh Century, and as it so affects the art of design in weaving throughout Europe, it is of the greatest interest. In its eastward expansion it seized Persia and India, Mesopotamia and Turkey. Spreading from Arabia eastward, it absorbed Egypt and North Africa, seizing

Sicily on the way, as it proceeded to Spain. The art canons of Islam, being affected with a rigidity based on religious beliefs, possessed marked ornament all its own. This it impressed—sometimes under pain of death—upon each conquered country. But as the countries conquered were highly developed in art, the Mohammedan frequently retained their design but put upon it the mark of his own religion's requirements, the arabesque, the geometric complexity, the introduction of Arab lettering.

Textiles of North Egypt, Spain, Sicily, Lucca and Venice, all in turn came under the influence of Mohammedan art, and received its impress. And this is one of the several ways in which European textiles received the enduring influence of the fertile Orient. We of the Western civilization must confess to a joyous satisfaction in the evidences of this influence. It is what made gorgeous the velvets of Genoa and Lucca, the brocades of Florence, the bewildering silk textiles of Venice, from the Thirteenth to the Sixteenth Centuries. And these have ever been the foundation of textile design, the greater in strength and interest as they came unaltered from the Orient.

CHAPTER III

EVER and ever the art of the East thrusts itself upon our notice in textiles. If the moment comes when one impatiently asks why our great European civilization went elsewhere for inspiration, there is but one way to find the answer, and that is to take a run over the history of the early centuries of our era. I imply haste in the glance because the history of those times is so fascinating and absorbing that textiles might well be forgot in observing the deep swing of race movements.

One cannot study textiles without knowing of the people who designed and wove and used them. It may be a blow to pride to accept the fact that Europe hung far behind in arts and letters during the centuries of the Dark Ages and into the Middle Ages. That period of retrogression and stagnancy was Europe's alone, hard as it is to acknowledge. The glorious East had no such period. It went on from century to cen-

33

tury without falling into darkness. Centers of government changed, and types of rulers, but learning and cultivation were ever present.

The best remains of the weaver's work that is not hopelessly effaced by time is the Coptic. If one were to choose a race to love and investigate, perhaps it would not be the Copts, that people who lived in Northern Egypt until Rome fell, and until the Caliphs of Islam came and ruled over them with the usual gentle ways of the conqueror.

But we cannot avoid giving them our best attention, because of the place they occupy in the world of textiles. To them and their mortuary customs we are indebted for the earliest specimens of weaving. It is unthinkable that their fabrics were the best in the world for the first centuries of our era, but theirs are almost the only ones that have not perished under the grinding foot of Time.

Accounts of marvelous hangings, of cushions, of clothing are not wanting. Greece and Rome have pictured theirs on vases, ancient literature tells of the luxury of stuffs in Babylonia and Persia while in India and China cave paintings are eloquent of drapings.

34

CHINESE SILKS IN THE FOURTEENTH CENTURY IM-
PORTED INTO ITALY INSPIRED SUCH RESTLESS DESIGNS
AS THESE BIRDS

ITALIAN, FOURTEENTH CENTURY, WHEN LUCCA CAME
UNDER THE INFLUENCE OF IMPORTATIONS OF CHI-
NESE TEXTILES

But of what practical use to us except as an interesting legend? All of this gorgeous wealth of weaving and embroidery disappeared centuries ago, but the Coptic textiles remained, if only in small pieces, because such were enclosed in enduring sarcophagi and neatly committed to the sand.

To the museum let us go and make friends with the Copts in a human sort of way. They kindly left their portraits, which we may gaze at with some degree of admiration and sympathy. With their friendly dark eyes and general youthfulness they excite a degree of interest, until Copt becomes a word that we possess as our own. These are of the people who wove designs Hellenic, Christian or Islamic according to the decree of their successive rulers.

Egypt is a natural museum because of the dry sands which have preserved the objects committed to their care. So when we slip among the aisles and ponder over the cases of our museums, we see the tunics and even the hangings that were tucked in among the wrappings of some athletic youth or lovely lady when they were comfortably laid away to await the day when the impish curiosity of the archeologist should expose these bits of textiles to the light. It is odd we are so shameless about this display. Will the day come when the burial places of New England will be critically dissected in the name of Puritan wedding rings, for instance? Were I an Egyptian I should hotly though humorously protest against my ancestors being exposed as specimens and their burial clothing as human documents.

Coptic weaves then give us the best of such treasures as are left from ancient days. Greece had her hangings and her flowing robes, but time has abolished them all. Rome the same, and China led them all with her silks, but scant are the remains left by wear and climate. A few bits of China's fabrics were buried under the sands of Chinese Turkestan's desert waiting for Sir Aurel Stein to dig them out with heart-thrills.

The Coptic weave for the best designs is the same as that used centuries later by weavers of tapestries in Europe, but executed with a fineness of texture never employed in European wall-hangings. These early pieces are always small, most frequently only ornaments to be sewn on a linen garment of some simple weave, but they are of a quality that represents patience beyond praise. They were executed during the Roman Empire probably by the slaves which were attached to a landed rich man's possessions.

It was from the Second to the Seventh Centuries that most of the Coptic pieces were made which are displayed in museums for the delectation of those who like to dig among the roots of the subject of weaving. Many of the Copts foreswore the old gods and goddesses of Roman myth and followed the Christ. But in the weaving of the marvelous bits of fabric that have recently been unearthed, the designs show sometimes the Hellenistic influence of Rome, as well as the symbols of the Christian, and also of the Moslem.

They must be seen in the hand that their technique and their beauty be revealed. The earliest ones were of but one color, dark blue, purple, brown, the pattern delicately outlined with a fine thread of white. Among these bits of solid color with outlined pattern are the interlaced geometric designs that have ever been associated with Saracen art.

Colors of many kinds were first used in the Third Century. Coptic fabrics in multicolor show the highest perfection in weaving and a technique that would have astonished French, Italian and Flemish weavers of tapestries in their highest moments of perfection. Shades melted into each other with the expedient of "hatching" until designs lost their look of flatness and took on the effect of having the three dimensions of length, breadth and especially of thickness. In other words modeling had appeared in woven figures.

Hellenistic designs came to the Copts as a part of the Roman culture of the day, and among these are figures of flying cupids, of the human figure, of lions, and of meanders and reciprocal borders like to those seen in the mosaics of a Roman palace floor.

These were made in the time when great religious confusion reigned, for the Roman Emperor ruled all of the Western World, Europe and even England. Christianity was gradually changing the thought of the rulers, and the new religion influenced the arts of the time. Christian art succeeded Roman, still carrying on Roman tradition, until the conquest of Islam and the invasion of the Northern Barbarians gave different impulse.

Our first Coptic pieces are Egyptian, of that late Egypt which had such close associations with the late

Greek and newer Roman ideals. Indigenous they were nevertheless. At this time a coarse weave prevailed, of looped threads, not unlike our Turkish toweling when done in the garments of linen or cotton, but Coptic ornamental weaving being usually in wool the effect of the loops was not unlike that in fine hooked rugs.

The second evidence bore the mark of the civilization across the Mediterranean which was now in possession of the country of the Copts. It is hard not to attribute these designs to Rome or to ancient Greece, but as Rome ruled all of the so-called Western World which included North Africa, it is but natural that Roman art had come with Roman legions. And there was Alexandria, that acme of classic cultivation established on Egyptian soil.

The time when the Copts were weaving their suave and colorful wool was one of the most worshipful of all the world's history. To look now at a map of the Roman Empire during the first centuries is to feel how simple and peaceful must political life have been with but one government over all of Europe, North Africa, Near East and Britain.

The Emperor was the undisputed ruler. There

were, to be sure, many millions of persons without drawing-room speech and manners, but it was cleverly arranged that teachers of the Greek and Latin classics abounded in every large town from end to end of the Empire. Thus the elect had a common language and common subjects of interest. And the man whose home was in Mesopotamia made instant friends with men met in London—provided his life was long enough to make the journey from the Euphrates to the Thames on horseback. All were citizens of a Roman world, and there could be no quarreling about buffer states and boundaries.

The Roman dominance went on for nearly five hundred years, this great political unity of all the world of Europe and beyond. Greek and Latin learning and art prevailed as the ideal of culture. Then new thoughts came in, a stiffening of old models when the Empire set up a capital in Byzantium, and the Near East was thus brought closer to Rome. Then came a division of power with two capitals, and then came the great movement of the Mohammedan conquest, then of the Barbarian Invasions which in course of time overthrew the Roman Empire and produced the suppression of learning which in turn produced the Dark Ages of Europe.

But lest we of European blood think only of Greco-Roman culture, turn again for a moment to the East, whose vitality never failed, whose luxury and riches encouraged lightness of life in the folk of Damascus, of Bagdad, of Persia—not forgetting the great Mohammedan leaders sweeping over from Arabia. Northern Barbarians were not riding down upon them from inexhaustible hordes. The people of the East were hunting and romancing just as ever, poignantly vicious, beautifully daring, ingeniously tyrannic.

The Arabian Nights Entertainment never fails to entertain. Even those who have no patience with history absorb it in these tales all unwittingly, for they are the myth and truth of centuries of Eastern culture. And among all these folk both mythical and real were the merchants ever carrying Oriental textiles from city to city, from inland to coast on long trains of camels.

The story of Mohammed seems unavoidable; therefore we rustle its pages and in so doing attach more romance to our textile designs. Not having been born in the atmosphere of Islam, we can take it lightly by

41

eliminating the religious aspect and by looking upon
Mohammed solely as a political leader and Empire
builder of astounding force. He was but a humble
young Arab when he listened to divine words in the
desert which he was crossing with packs of merchan-
dise on a slow-moving camel-train. Yet in but a short
time he was established in sacred Mecca, so powerful
and rich that his enemies—after the manner of such—
sought to kill him.

He then made his flight to Medina, the Hegira.
This date is 622, and was elected to be the year one in
Islam's calendar. Perhaps it was this forced retire-
ment from the city of wealth, perhaps it was a remembrance of his camel-train days when he became aware
of the riches of other countries as shown by their merchants, but however it was, Mohammed decided to
gather his men about him and embark on a series of
conquests. It seemed a magnificent project, to give
the countries of the East a new ruler who should in
conquering give them the true religion.

In pursuit of territory and glory his hunger grew.
Syria was the first bite, then Egypt, Asia Minor, Sicily,
and at last all of Northern Africa reaching to where

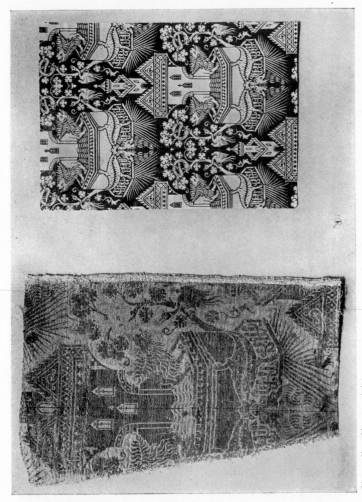

LUCCA SILK (AND COPY) FOURTEENTH CENTURY, MINGLING CHINESE BIRDS
AND RAYS, ARAB TEXT, AND PERSIAN LIONS, FAVORITE TRADITIONS OF THE
WIDE EAST

PERSIAN FIGURED SILK WITH DESIGN OF A PERSIAN
LEADING A MONGOL PRISONER THROUGH A COUNTRY
FILLED WITH DOMESTIC ANIMIALS.   SIXTEENTH CEN-
TURY

it took but one leap of the seven-league-boots to spring over to Gibraltar, and so on through rugged smiling Spain.

The Saracens—as the Arabs were called in Europe—took Spain when it was wild and undeveloped, made of it a Caliphate of Cordova and flooded it with culture and beauty, *vide* the Alhambra still left on Granada's hill. As for the university and library at Cordova, history alone can tell of them, for the rich and intellectual town of the Mohammedans is gone over to sadness and poverty—all save the gorgeous mosque to enter which is to wander in a forest of Allah, so like a mystic wood is the crowd of pillars holding its low arches. Before condemning all this as extraneous to the matter in hand, think further and note the effect of this bit of history on design, which includes designs for textiles.

Long before Spain was securely under the Moslem's dominance, Egypt was in his hand. The Arabs there fell into a magnificent luxury which had immense influence on the Coptic weavers. First was the effect on design to which allusion has been made. Mohammed was over-meticulous about design, and forced it

43

into an elaboration of geometrics, forbidding representations of animate forms. But the Coptic weavers had these last already in their repertory and at their able finger-tips, so notwithstanding the command of new masters they continued some of the old Christian and Hellenic conventions.

There was attached to the law an uncomfortable proviso, that in case a Mohammedan wore a garment, or used a hanging displaying the objects offensive to Mohammed's taste, he was to be at once dispatched to another world where he might meditate on his sins during aeons of torture. Human imagination ever seems to display this sort of invention at times of great religious fervor. The figures forbidden were those of mankind and other animate life as well as portraits.

But when the able weavers of Egypt produced such magnificent cloths as the conquerors had never seen, many bearing the offense against the Prophet, a way out had to be found, for to burn such noble furnishings were unthinkable. Christians in those days being quite accustomed to suffering, Islam made new decrees whereby the designs of the fabrics should bring the tortures of hell upon the *weavers* and not the *owners*.

44

Thus the caliphs accept such pieces of weaving as are preserved by history, though unhappily the eye will never see them more.

Tents and their hangings, they were, the houses and furnishings of great men who traveled in those climes and in those days. We hear of one tent so large that seventy camels were needed for its transport. It was entirely lined with silks. Alexandria fell to the Caliph Omar in 641 and we can fancy the treasure there.

When the Mohammedans found their capital Medina too small a city, in too arid a country, for the capital of a conquering nation, Damascus was occupied, and after that Bagdad. And here again are names to conjure with, names that dazzle with their jewels, that bring out princesses, houris, thieves, lovers, tyrants, all the inspiring puppets of Eastern tales to make us their happy slaves in meditation. Persia itself was not exempt. By the year 750 A.D. the Mohammedan Conquest reached from India to the Atlantic. If one has a firm hold on mental clarity, one can think of the effect which this great conquest of the East and West had on Islamic art.

As time went on the Coptic figures underwent a

slow decadence. Outlines were feebler and motives became fretted with useless details, while animals grew unbeautifully grotesque. And in all of this was historic reason. Damascus, that great Islamic center of trade, was supplying merchants of the West with goods brought there from Persia, and the strange designs were distantly copied and mutilated in the Coptic weaving. They can sometimes be recognized by the use of the figures, Persian figures, the tree-of-life and the altar of fire. Besides this was the introduction of hunting scenes, represented usually with a mounted hunter and a single animal. All of these are traced to Persia.

The uses of these Coptic fabrics? As said before they are of use to us only in the enchantment of connecting history with the art of woven designs. On the day when these delicious bits were in actual use, they represented the adornment and decoration of succeeding races in North Africa.

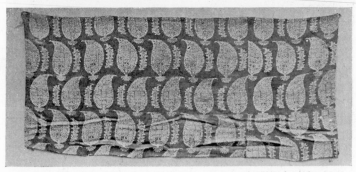

SPANISH-MOORISH SILK WITH DESIGNS LIKE THOSE ON
TILES. (*Below*) PERSIAN BROCADE OF CLASSIC PATTERN,
EIGHTEENTH CENTURY

PERSIAN VELVET, SIXTEENTH CENTURY. DETAIL OF
HUNTING SCENE FROM A TENT CEILING PROBABLY
OWNED BY SOLEIMAN THE MAGNIFICENT (1520-1566).
ONLY IN PERSIA WERE SUCH ELABORATE PATTERNS
WOVEN IN VELVET

CHAPTER IV

WERE I a Spaniard with a name denoting Arab blood, my pride would be insufferable because of the cultivation brought to Spain by the Saracen. What was Europe in the Eighth and Ninth Century? A waste in which crouched dumb races, either fallen from the recently banished Roman Culture or never having developed.

And what was the culture of the Mohammedan? It was such that it led the world in science and carried with it an art of exquisite development and permanent beauty. It was the intent of Islam to improve the regions of which it became possessed through conquest, to establish there not only its religion but its culture.

The Moors having entered there, Spain was the chief European country, that was blooming intellectually in the Eighth Century, establishing universities, building marvelously beautiful mosques and palaces, and ornamenting all with an art peculiarly its own. The Moors were driven from Spain in 1492 when Boabdil breathed

47

sadly, *"l'ultimo sospiro del Moro,"* and left the field of
art and learning to the Christians. Naturally it was
the first duty of the conquering Christians to destroy
that art and learning. But never did the new power
succeed in obliterating the spirit of Moorish art in
Spain, and thus the ornament of that alluring country
has ever differed from that of the rest of Europe.

Grateful let us be that the conquerors in obliterating
Grenada left the Alhambra. If inclined to resent the
presence there of the big Renaissance building erected
before it by Charles V one must think on that Emperor's tolerance in leaving the rest of the palace as it
was built by the Moors. And happy are we that in
destroying the university of Cordova the new in power
left the wondrous mosque.

Putting these great examples with the palace of the
Alcázar and the Giralda tower in Seville, we have a
complete education in the Moorish design that colors
all Spanish ornament that is truly of Spain and not a
direct importation from Italy's Renaissance.

Take a few days off and loaf among them and see
what can be absorbed in a little time. Arabesques, of
course, geometric designs and interlacings which are

48

the peculiar touch of Mohammedan art in its purity. But with what fine intellectual quality these arabesques are invested. Their variety is infinite, their meanderings exquisite, and they seem ever to speak of life itself, the life of luxury and cultivation led by the elegant and fastidious Moors in this European Caliphate of Cordova.

As you meditate, people of those times come to life, and the palaces are dressed in Oriental richness as a soft background for slender figures, gauze-draped, who lounge among the rugs and cushions, who mistily wander among the columns, who listen thrilled to the beat of distant Arab music, who throw a rose from a draped balcony. Othello and Desdemona become real, and Ferdinand and Isabella invite your hatred.

As one discovers the arabesques in fabrics woven during the three centuries after the banishment of the Arab, and is able thus to say of a strange exotic ornament, "Ah, this is old Spanish," so in the pure arabesques themselves, as drawn by the Moors, there is the trace of yet older ornaments.

And thus an extra fascination invests the fabrics. Persia is found to have contributed the leaf which lies flat in a trefoil and when doubled makes the ornament yet more pointed and graceful as it bends on curving stems. From Persia, too, comes the cone-shaped flower which began as a pomegranate and grew in Turkey almost to a fan in size. The design of four flowers became a classic, a central rose surrounded by a hyacinth, tulip, carnation, all with long curved stems. And the truly Mohammedan motive of interlaced lines excites admiration by its variety. All these motives are familiar in all silk weaves. Arabic lettering, too, was judiciously woven in. To these add the color of the Orient, the daring use of color for its inspirational value, and you have the key to Spanish textiles.

Remembering that the Mohammedan caliphs invaded Persia while Persia was one of the centers of art, it is easy to see the reasons for these designs. The Moslems in conquering adopted the art of the conquered, rather than creating one of their own, thus writing their history into their ornament. Without these outside influences Moslem art with its geometric patterns and interwoven designs of straight lines would have become arid in the course of centuries. But Persia gave her lovely use of flowers with their endless possibilities

and poetic suggestions. There is magic in the words—
a Persian garden; it makes one think of tinkling fountains, perfumes, moonlight,—and those who walked
therein—clandestinely or otherwise.

But before the Moors had been part-banished, part-
suppressed the pattern set by Italy was being followed.
The Renaissance was Italy. The whole of Europe was
on the upward trend, but in Italy was the great development. It was not the gift of some conqueror belonging to a higher culture, but was a development of
self. And after Italy had evolved the new kingdom of
science and art, the crudeness of the Middle Ages gradually disappeared in country after country.

But each country which adopted the art of Italy in
the Fifteenth and Sixteenth Centuries, wove into the
designs some motive peculiar to themselves, or some
local color scheme. Spain at the time of Ferdinand and
Isabella was not entirely Moorish. Christian influence
from the North had been steadily encroaching on the
power of the Moslem and with its political advance
came its art. And that was the art of Italy's Renaissance.

Velvets, brocades and damasks woven at that time in

51

Spain are only distinguishable from the Italian product when they show the touch of the Moor. Spain produced more and more rich fabrics, the demand for them became extraordinary not only among the royalty and the nobles but among the rich men of business affairs; and many of these textiles are in our hands today.

We are dealing with a most exciting time in history, for events in Spain in 1492 are intimately connected with "these United States of America." Columbus sailed then by the grace of Their Most Catholic Majesties, Ferdinand and Isabella. Navigation was one of the freest movements of the Renaissance. All persons of intelligence knew then that the world was not flat but spherical. And all navigators and merchants hoped to find a shorter way to the Isles of Spice and to the wealth of Inde than the trade-routes over the land.

Spice seemed to be a puny motive for perilous adventure, cinnamon and cloves and pepper a small reward for danger, until one remembers that spice not only enlivened the dull stews of the early days but they preserved perishable food. The frigidaire was yet to come. Marco Polo's accounts of spice in the markets of the

Moluccas and Ceylon lured many a sailor from home and fireside. In 1486 Diaz rounded the Cape of Good Hope. In 1498 Vasco da Gama followed that path and traced it still further, sailing straight across the Indian Ocean to Hindustan; and Magellan soon after sailed right around the world.

But these accomplishments counted less with Spain than the discoveries in America, for the new world was annexed as Spanish territory and from it she drew wealth that seemed to be inexhaustible. On this she grew to greatness and power, and a royal daughter of Spain was desired by Maximilian as wife for his son Philip, and from this marriage was born the Emperor Charles V, whose story involves the whole of Europe.

Gold from the new world was then in every Spaniard's pockets. The royal treasury bulged with it, and extravagance was lauded, not rebuked. And among things produced for church, for home, for personal use were the magnificent textiles. The walls of churches and of palaces were hung with damasks, and embroiderers were set to work on altar cloths and clerical vestments such as amaze us of today. It was sufficient glory for the aristocratic family of Covarrubias to be known as the best embroiderers in the kingdom. Much gold was woven into fabrics and stitched into vestments and clothing. Heaviness rather than delicacy was characteristic. Portraits of the time show skirts that must have been a burden of great weight. The lightsome step of youthful maids must have been suppressed by such heavy volume of riches in brocade.

Thus Spain spent her money easily that came so easily. "Savages" in Peru, in Central America, in Mexico yielded up their mines and golden images under the gentle persuasion of the sword. And while the supply lasted Spain was a great power with a great commerce in textiles.

And just here we stumble upon an evidence of weaving in one of the countries of the new world—Peru, that home of a developed race which was taken over about 1530 in the name of Spain by the adventurer Pizarro. Chronologically it has no place here except as a discovery of Spain during the Renaissance.

Peruvian weaving is placed as far back as the Third Century of our era. Beautiful cloths, perfect in preservation, are dated as far back as the Tenth Century. One of the piquant puzzles of the history of weaving is the similarity between the Peruvian product and the Coptic. Both are preserved in burial places—or none would be remaining. Both are of the weave adopted by tapestry makers of Europe. The Peruvians, however, have the distinction of a technique in weaving, a certain twisting of the warp, that brings despair to the heart of the archeologist who would reconstruct the Peruvian loom.

The ornament is that of people who picture nature symbolically, many birds or fishes being seen in repetition. The swastika, the fret, are such as are found among all primitive or fundamental art. The dyes are gay, red and ivory tones predominating, and time has not hurt their colors. We stand before them amazed. They are the great enigma in the world of textiles. They were woven contemporaneously with the Coptic, of the same stitch, yet a world apart in "locale" and in tradition of ornament. It was the Incas who destroyed these South American people and these were in power when Spain appeared, and took over the country which they named "Peru."

If the collector or even the student can airily dismiss from his mind the real object of a tomb, he can become thrilled over the archeologist's treasure unearthed in Peru—still being unearthed. The strange burial customs of ancient Peru demanded large quantities of textiles enclosed within the huge bundle which contained the mummy.

As has been said, these are mainly woven in a technique identical with that of the tapestry weavers among the Copts (during the same centuries) and of the European tapestry weavers whose work flowered a few centuries later. The color gamut too is noticeably similar.

Thus these newly discovered textiles are the excitement of the day among archeologists and textile collectors. It is easy to see the reason. So few very ancient textiles are in existence, that this large and sudden addition thrills the searcher after evidences of the past.

Peru has now been divided into districts for search, and into the periods, pre-Inca and Inca. The tapestry weave is not the only one found, the designs are archaic, the dates are from obscure times until 1200, when the Incas conquered the native, and from then until Pizarro the Spaniard took a conqueror's possession of the country.

While still thinking on Spain, her conquests and royal extravagances, her art and at last her decay, it is agreeable to remember that in the Seventeenth Century she produced artists beyond the ideals of the time. It was a century of decadence in Italy; the bud had opened, the flower had bloomed, and now the wide-expanded petals were falling. But in Spain Velasquez had arisen, and through all that century there were others, Murillo, Ribera, and El Greco, the Greek Theotocopuli who brought with him the Byzantine tradition.

As is ever the case the lesser arts were influenced by the greater, and textiles in Spain during the Seventeenth Century showed tremendous vigor in design. Not only were the large motives continued, but there were introduced the fine-woven small figures sprinkled over a plain background which are in direct contrast to the older ornament. And ever a reminiscence of the Moor appeared in a detail or in color.

CLOTH OF GOLD

Cloth of gold spread its glittering surface over all countries of Europe in the time of the Renaissance, and even prior to that. One cannot think of Persia without it, and Asia Minor and Turkey were sources of supply in the years before the Renaissance. To Cyprus and Lucca are attributed the cloth of gold supplied to kings of Europe from the Fourteenth to Sixteenth Centuries.

It seems to have been regarded as inseparable from events of State. Kings and queens were dressed in cloth of gold, and returning victors had their horses enveloped in it. A king of England, even before the Tudors, must use it lavishly at his coronation to be appropriately impressive, and the richer nobles must follow suit.

An English king in those days must blazen with gold and bright color. Before the ceremony he must find himself in the Tower, where a ritual bath was taken in preparation in a room made elegant by this same cloth of gold, even the carved stone bath being draped with it. The king himself was burdened with as many golden robes as his youthful frame could well support, and then he began a royal progress from the Tower to the Abbey at Westminster. Ten yards of cloth of gold might dress the king, and ten more were required for the flowing cover of the horse he rode. The king's garments were of purple, the "trappour" of his horse were crimson, mingled with the gold. The queen chose white brocaded on the gold, and reclined on cushions of the same, while her maids and their carriages were draped in crimson and gold. Everywhere along the way were banners waving and draperies hung from windows, and many of these were of this same rich cloth of gold.

The Abbey itself at a coronation shone with gorgeousness. Even the tombs of kings were made gay by a covering of cloth of gold. A high stage was built for the new king's chair, canopied and draped with cloth of gold, and the chair of the archbishop was similarly decorated. After the coronation the king and queen proceeded to Westminster Hall for the banquet, and there the same gorgeous cloth of gold was draped against the wall to make a dorser or back to the royal seats. Such pageantry must be recalled to dress the Abbey and the Great Hall of Westminster as they were dressed in other days. If nowadays the informal behavior and dress of ministers and members in the Hall offend, let the mind glow with remembrance of former customs there—forgetting perhaps that men in those other more gorgeous days *rode* in among the august company if the fancy led them. And if the dreary crowd of monuments in the Abbey press too hard upon the spirits, forget their artistic failure and see in their place the glowing canopies and drapings of the past.

England was not making stuffs of such richness at that time. It all came to her from outside, and much of it from the Near East, from Turkey, for example. The designs show this, the ornament being the over-sized floral motives that have ever characterized that district. As soon as Italy had acquired knowledge and practise of the silk industry, she, too, wove cloth of gold and supplied in great part the almost barbaric display which was the weakness of kings and the demand of the populace.

The cloth of gold of the Fourteenth Century and immediately after was not always one glittering sheet of woven metal as the name implies, but was brocaded in showy figures of silk or velvet which added enormously to the beauty of the material. The designs were the same as those large ones used in silken fabrics which originated in the Near East. The pomegranate, the artichoke, the undulating band of ornament which, crossing with its mate, formed a frame for a central floral motive. These same fabrics were made during the Renaissance with but little change, and some of these are still beautifying rich interiors. And if we may not drape them over beds or cover with them a prancing steed, we may at least revel in their beauty and in memory of their halcyon days.

One of the historic pictures which seems to depend on textiles for its fame, however much man himself may exceed in value the product of his hands, is the celebrated meeting of the three superlative monarchs of France, England and Austria—Francis I, Henry VIII, Charles V, on the Field of the Cloth of Gold. It may be a shock to the romantic department of one's mind to read on the pamphlet of the "Golden Arrow" train to Paris from London that the historic golden country was the countryside just south of Calais, which now seems utterly lacking in interest and beauty. But here it was that the monarchs met, all young and handsome, to form (ostensibly) a fraternity which should smooth the path to glory and not redden it with blood as was the usual way. Yet for all their kingly honor,

61

there was trouble within a year, when Charles the young emperor, who had inherited much and had married into Spain, thought it polite to pursue the gay young Francis of artistic cultivation that Charles might include France in his ever widening empire.

It was a gorgeous meeting, for no matter how simple a spot had been chosen for convenience' sake, the scene was made indescribably brilliant by the display of cloth of gold used in every possible way as decoration, in banners, in canopies, in drapings wherever draping was possible.

Manufacture has half spoiled such scenes for us. Cloth of gold is now as common as silken fabrics. We know how to weave it by machine; we know how to substitute baser metals for the precious ones, so that every woman may have many golden dresses in her wardrobe, and may hang golden cloths at her windows. And thus it comes that the cheaper products have made us think of such display as crudely theatric.

But then it was almost solid metal unalloyed, skilfully wound on a core of silk or cotton to make a thread which it was possible to weave. Does not one hear of

62

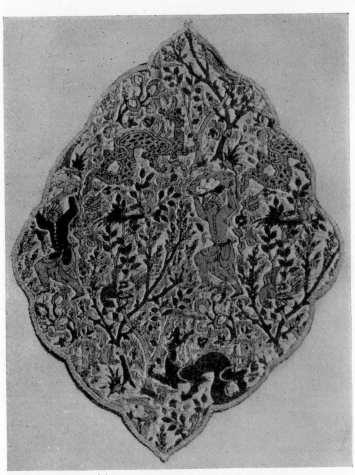

PERSIAN VELVET 1540, GOLD THREAD. A HUNTER HURLS A
ROCK AT A DRAGON OF CHINESE INVENTION

PERSIAN BROCADE OF THE SEVENTEENTH
CENTURY WITH VELVET FIGURES ON A
GROUND OF GOLD

old hangings or clothing being burned that the gold metal woven into them might be regained to use again? And the weaving, too, was done on hand looms, adding great expense of labor to expense of material.

The Middle Ages gave free use of color, and bright color was carried over into the Renaissance, and the times favored the cloth of gold for its pageantry—for what else but pageantry were the ceremonies of the Doge of Venice, or the visit of a Medici to a Sforza, or the crowning of a king, or a significant meeting of three monarchs?

Spain, oddly enough, sought gold in the new world to spend it on goods imported from Genoa and Venice, the gold-woven fabrics with which to dazzle her friends and enemies. Her industries at home were all neglected while she drew on the supply of gold and silver which had been discovered in the new world of America. All the merchant adventurers of Europe knew Spain as a market for the rich stuffs of Italy and the East, and thither they sailed with full ships, taking in return the gold which was more scarce in their lands than in Spain. Even England worked up a tre-

mendous commerce with her cloths, which she skilfully unloaded in all the Spanish ports.

Masters of vessels were given royal commands to
dispose, each voyage, of a given number of pieces of
cloth in Spain, even though their cargo was of raw
materials. And thus early the coffers of England received the benefit of gold drawn from the Americas
by Spain.

The textiles of England were mainly of wool. As
she absorbed the culture of the Renaissance, she began
to make the silken fabrics, and the later cotton weaves,
but the foundation of her ancient trade was wool, and
in this matter she came in close touch with Flanders.
And here again appears more history. Many of the
weavers of France were of the Protestant faith in the
Sixteenth Century, Huguenots. In the religious conflicts they fled to Flanders for protection and there pur-
sued their craft. When in 1598 the King, Henri IV,
issued the Edict of Nantes, giving protection to Protestants, many refused to return to France, and later
settled in England. Thus England became the wool-
weaving center of the world. And this industry
formed the base on which Queen Elizabeth built up
her nation's commerce.

CHAPTER V

WITHOUT silk as the weaver's thread, the story of textiles would lose its glamour. It was this marvelous material that made possible the translation of the design into fabrics of surpassing beauty and inspired artists to still nobler compositions. Myth and history blend in their usual charm to preserve a story of the discovery of silk, for it might be called a discovery as well as a development. The story goes that four thousand years ago an empress of China, reposing and poetizing among the flowers of her garden, saw on a leaf of her mulberry tree, a group of pale greenish worms of infinitesimal size hungrily devouring the succulent foliage. Being of tender heart, she refrained from having the creatures stamped out of existence by the foot of her attendant. The next week she again took a peep at the fascinating though repellent sight and found that the tiny worms had grown preposterously in the interim and had spread over the tree in search of pastures new. Their feeding capacity was abnormal except on one day at the end of each week's time, when they grew slothful, refused food and cast their skins, which were then uncomfortably tight. Even though her favorite mulberry tree was becoming bare, she suffered that annoyance to observe the habits of the worms. At last came a day when the worms began to turn to a translucent yellow, and to wrap themselves in a fine thread which flowed from the mouth. The cocoon being complete, and the Empress endowed with patience, she had the ultimate pleasure of seeing a butterfly emerge and in its turn lay the eggs which produced yet more worms. Anybody might have done as much as this, but it is believed that the Empress Si-Ling-Shi was the first to experiment with the cocoons and to discover that the thread of which they were made could be unwound (better if the pupæ were still within) and spun into a yarn from which the weavers made fabrics more lovely than any in the world.

China is the country of silk. When sericulture was first commenced is lost in the mist of centuries long before the Christian Era. The story of the Empress

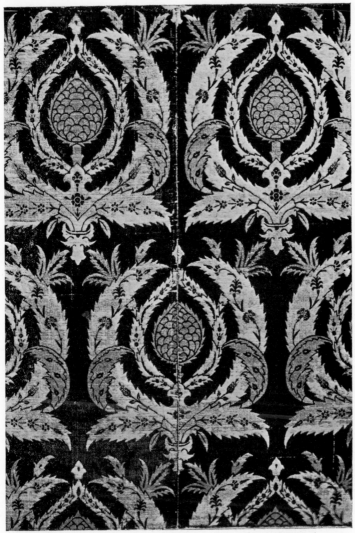

TURKISH BROCADED VELVET OF THE FIFTEENTH CEN-
TURY. PATTERN OF A VARIANT OF POMEGRANATE
WITH PALM FOLIAGE

ITALIAN VELVET, 1450 TO 1500, WITH CURVED
BANDS AND ARTICHOKES, MOTIVES WHICH CAME
FROM THE EAST

Si-Ling-Shi—2640 B.C.—makes a pretty legend even though it be only legend, but the fact is established that the cultivation of the silkworm began in China and existed there and there only for many centuries before it was introduced to other countries.

All records of old travelers in the East speak with delight of the marvelous silken textiles of China on which flowers bloom as in a garden, and which it is a luxury to pass through the hand. The Chinese themselves were clothed entirely in silk. To other peoples it was a marvel, for the materials of their fabrics was wool, linen or cotton.

China knew the value of her silk, she had abundant proof from other nations that all the world desired it. And she therefore guarded the secret of sericulture and silk weaving. That the two are distinct and separate industries helped China to retain for many centuries her unique position.

Sericulture relates to the worm and his care. It might be said that primarily it relates to the mulberry tree. Where that refuses to grow and put out succulent leaves the worm cannot produce the cocoon of high grade, for the silkworm feeds solely upon those leaves. This tree, which is shorn of its leaves for the worm as a sheep is shorn of his wool, grows only in mild climates where it can revive and grow fresh leaves after the season of the worm's appetite is past.

Whether or not the original silkworm observed by the Empress Si-Ling-Shi was the self-indulgent and tender creature of today, we cannot know, but he seems like any highly bred animal in his demands for special food, even temperature and no draughts, and he also needs the offices of a gentle hand if he feels languid when the time comes for spinning his cocoon. And his size for a worm is prodigious.

All wrapped in his self-made silk he becomes the commercial cocoon, but still he occupies the attention of his servitors, for he must not die until he is taken to the place where human hands may unwrap him with almost as much skill as he employed in the enveloping. His intention of emerging as a butterfly ends with his immersion in hot liquid. A few of his kind are allowed to live that eggs may be supplied for the next crop of cocoons.

In old China the work then went into the hands of deft maids who found the glued end of the worm's thread and reeled it off as one reels cotton from a spool. The process thus begun ends in the woven textile, but first the thread is spun, composed of varying numbers of the worm's filament according to the thickness required. In modern parlance this is called the yarn.

That the first silk fabrics were Chinese is a fact of history, but none of them remain to show us their beauty. We owe to the explorations of Sir Aurel Stein a bit of silk of the Han Dynasty (206 B.C. to 220 A.D.). The earliest examples show a surprisingly beautiful blending of the Chinese and the Hellenistic in the woven figures.

Taking into consideration the exigencies of sericulture and the niceties of metamorphosing the cocoon into a weavable thread for the loom, it is easily seen why China could keep her secret and was for so many centuries the source of silk.

Silk weaving is recorded by all countries of the East, but sericulture remained exclusively China's. Other lands were forced, in order to possess the prized material, to buy from China the silk thread all ready for the loom, or the cocoons from which to make the threads. Over the trade routes the Chinese then sent their shimmering silks, their cocoons and their silken yarn. But sericulture was theirs alone.

Aristotle speaks of silk. Gauze of Cos was famous in the time of Alexander the Great. Perhaps the veils of Salome were made of it. Rome had woven silks but worth their weight in gold when it came to purchasing. Persia, India, both close to China, wove in silk. Egypt in the north had silks woven by the Copts in the early centuries of our era. China furnished the product of the silkworm for all of these.

The secrets of China gradually leaked out. Credence is given to the manner of their reaching Japan about 300 A.D. and Byzantium the capital of the Eastern Empire in 550, under the Emperor Justinian. Japan sent some Koreans to China to engage silk instructors. The result was their persuading four Chinese girls to return with them to Japan and teach the processes necessary for figure weaving of silk. Byzantium received instructions from two Persian Nestorian monks in 550 whose adventures smack of the dishonorable. Having traveled as holy men through China, they learned there the processes of sericulture. It was comparatively a simple matter, though an overt, to conceal within their pilgrim staves the silkworm's eggs and the seed of the mulberry. With these they left China and reached Byzantium. Thereafter in that city silk production rose high, and spread both east to Asia Minor and Syria, and west to Europe. India under the Mongols in 1525 reached her highest point in silk production. Persia under Shah Abbas (1586-1625) developed her most exquisite silks.

The figure of Shah Abbas stands out brilliantly in the history of Persian art. After the Sassanian kings came centuries that we skip with easy indifference, but in the reign of this famous man there occurred a revival of the arts and of poetry, and among it all a fresh supply of motives for silken fabrics. It is useless to praise their beauty on the printed page, one must see the actual examples to understand the patient talent and talented patience that produced these lovely results. This was the time when patterns were made with slim youths and maids dallying among the trees of the Persian gardens, armed with musical instruments for enchantment instead of the older arrow aimed at a wild animal of the hunt. A simpler pattern but full of poetic suggestion is the nightingale and the rose, which recalls the story of the bird's adoration of the flower with the deadly thorn.

It is said that a grandfather of Shah Abbas sent artist weavers into China to learn the magic of the looms in that country of silk, and that these men returning brought a memory of Chinese motives and reproduced them. Thus we see the cloud-motive and the dragon creep into Persian fabrics.

Tradition agrees that the worms' eggs did leave China by a trick, and sericulture began in the Near East and Europe. Thenceforth Europe had in her hand the perfect material for executing the marvelous wealth of design which began with the Gothic, glorified the Renaissance, beautified the brilliant Eighteenth Century and now—we come suddenly upon artificial silk which emerges like the genii from the bottle and fills the sky.

Remembering the astounding spread of the Moslem Empire, it is easy to see the Mohammedan carrying with him the silken textiles, introducing their manufacture into Sicily, when Palermo became the center of European silks in the Tenth to the Thirteenth Centuries, with weavers from the Orient and designs both Sassanian and Byzantine.

And it is easy to see that as the new craft came from the Islamic East it brought with it the ornament, the pine of India, the animals and flowers of Persia. Thus Byzantine designs and those of Sicily bear close resemblance.

The silks of Sicily were woven by migrating craftsmen from Persia and India, and they, too, contributed a share of old tradition. The birds and beasts of their invention are among the most entrancing ever woven. The Sicilians freed their groups from the encircling roundel or ogival band and threw them into the liberty of an ornamented space.

Silk went appropriately and naturally to Italy, where in the Thirteenth Century its manufactory was extensive. Venice took it easily from Constantinople, and Lucca took it from Sicily. Venice was partly under the domination of the Near East, and Sicily was taken by Charles of Anjou for the French in 1266. Sicilian weavers then fled to Lucca, where were developed those astounding designs of pomegranates and leaf motives continued by Florence after Lucca's brief flowering.

The Moslem took silk to Spain, and with it his especial and peculiar ornament which prevailed for centuries and is pleasantly detected in the design of today.

All Europe was draped with magnificent products of the silk looms in the Sixteenth Century. Every ruler who had in him the generous heart of a "father of his country," chafed at enriching other nations by importations and yearned to make of sericulture an industry of his people. Francis I of France brought mulberry trees and silkworms to the valley of the Rhone and there fostered the imported culture. But his venture could not last, and Lyons silk developed under imported raw material.

Under Louis XIV, Colbert with his widespread efficiency made the same experiment, but that also failed. Italy and the East still supplied cocoons and thread, as they do now.

England under James I made her experiment with mulberries and worms, but the climate killed the endeavor. Although failing in sericulture England was rich in weavers, and came to a high place in the manufacture of silk. In 1697 the importation of French silks

74

TURKISH VELVET OF SIXTEENTH CENTURY WITH
BOLD DESIGN OF TULIPS

ITALIAN VELVET FIFTEENTH CENTURY, SO-CALLED
GOTHIC VELVET WITH POMEGRANATE ENCLOSED IN
LEAF FORM

was prohibited and in 1701 those from China, India and Persia.

Weavers seemed the special marks for the arrows of misfortune and the frequent edicts of thrones drove them from one part of Europe to another. Thus they came to England. In 1585 the Spanish who ruled the fate of the Low Countries so persecuted the able Protestant weavers of that district that they fled to the more peaceable England. Add to this in 1685 the influx of French weavers who fled from the persecutions let loose by the Revocation of the Edict of Nantes, and England was magnificently equipped with weavers of silk.

The establishment of Spitalfields grew to occupy the first place in Europe, as Lyons declined by reasons of the flight of the weavers from religious persecution. French ability in silk weaving, French art in design were thus transplanted across the channel. Spitalfields workers like the weavers of Lyons had their looms at home. The masters supplied them with materials and designs, they delivered the textile all ready for use.

One great and primary difference between the silks woven of early Eastern design and those of Europe in the high days of Lyons and Spitalfields is that the Oriental relied for effect on the nobility of his design, which he expressed in few weaves while the European looked to compel admiration by the variety and intricacy of his weaves, letting the design take secondary place. In the Eighteenth Century the displaying of craftsmanship was the first consideration. This is the secret of the charm which resides in those old silks of Eastern design, that they ever delight the eye and stimulate the spirit, and this is accomplished—as in the Sassanian and the Byzantine—by adhering to robust forms, noble lines and adapted symbol.

It is not time wasted to pass an hour among frayed and fragile remains of the old silks of Eastern tradition, for therein is found a clue to some of the modernistic designs composed by the decorators of today. Consciously or unconsciously they incorporate the age-old motives in their newest drawings which thus gain in force and reason.

CHAPTER VI

EFFECTS OF EARLY RENAISSANCE

LET us look a bit at the textile industry of the early Renaissance in Italy, for Italy's Renaissance reached every department of art and erudition and put her products above those of other lands until they learned the trick from her.

Silk culture was well established, a momentous fact. None of the gorgeous fabrics of fine design which have for centuries delighted us could have been made had China been able to keep her secrets of sericulture. The new industry made all possible. As a result artists of high cultivation and talent put themselves to making patterns for the loom. Among these was so great a painter as the Venetian Jacopo Bellini. His designs are a joy to look upon because in them is displayed the intricacy of design ever loved by Venetians, in which is introduced a distinctly Oriental drawing. The reasons for that lie in the adventures of commerce between Europe and the Ottoman Empire, and the reli-

gious fervor which led to the Crusades. Each class of
designs as it appears is not the fancy or fashion of the
moment; it is a veritable human document, and records for him who can read the events of the time in
which it was made.

Among them all we stand fixed when the eye lights
on the specimens called Saracen, for these are full of
fine movement, exotics in their way and piquant with
interest, for they combine motives of Persia, India,
China. One cannot of course make use of Saracenic
fabrics in the home for the scant and fragile cloths that
remain to us are entirely unpractical for modern use
and are also gathered long since into such museums as
that at Lyons, the Galleria degli Arrazzi at Florence
and the Victoria and Albert in London. It is their influence that counts; their children live after them in
the perpetuating of their conventions in ornament.

Notwithstanding the arrogance of Europe towards
the peoples to the east of them, the dwellers in Mesopotamia, Turkey, Asia Minor, these had developed an
art in design that Europe was pleased to adopt. At
the time when Lucca was in possession of silk as a
weaving material, about 1200 A.D. there was much use

VELVET FROM ASIA MINOR, SIXTEENTH CENTURY.
OGIVAL DESIGN ENCLOSING CARNATIONS

ITALIAN VELVET OF THE FIFTEENTH CENTURY,
POMEGRANATE PATTERN

of Saracenic designs coming to her from Venice and Sicily.

These designs were marked by the use of pairs of animals either facing each other or the reverse. The animals always have a fantastic flavor which puts them at once into the land of faërie but in reality these designs are antique Persian or Sassanian, which were adopted by the Saracens. And all drawings are in two dimensions with the naïve flat look of mere pattern.

It might seem useless to dwell on silks so rare that they exist only in fragments, and serve no purpose in the home of today, were it not that we find in these interesting bits the origin of certain designs that have served through several centuries with alterations. It was from Persian influence through the Saracenic that the originals came of the patterns which enclose the figure in a frame, making a large medallion, round, polygonal or ogival. This was formed of a narrow border circling or meandering to cross with its mate. The whole surface of the cloth was covered thus. Saracen in the Middle Ages meant the Mohammedan of Europe and the Near East, therefore the Saracenic designs carried the flavor of the Mohammedan religious tradition. Each country conquered supplied new motives, and we see Persian and Indian ornament in Saracenic and in Byzantine silk.

Full of suggestion is the fact that some of these designs found their way to the looms of Italy and France through the medium of the Crusades. The Mussulman of the Near East, being in possession of the cradle of Christianity, the city of Jerusalem, it seemed a necessary and noble act for Christians to wrest the place from his defiling hand.

It is hard to mention the word Crusades without letting a vagrant mind wander off into journeyings of long-cloaked knights, invariably tall, commanding and inspired, and to follow them with the magnificent Richard Cœur de Lion to deeds of valor all combined with Eastern delights.

But the religious aspect of the Crusades is for the student of history. Our interest in the subject of textiles is better served if we direct a discerning eye upon the merchant of the day. Never once considering himself an artist nor thinking of supplying designs for weavers in Christian countries, he admirably filled these functions.

To the merchant of the big trading cities of Italy, Venice, Pisa, Genoa, as well as Constantinople, the Crusades spelled Opportunity, as we say in modern jargon. They first offered—doubtless at good prices— their merchant fleet for the transport of the knights from Italy to the ports of Palestine and Syria.

Once in these parts the merchants like the knights were amazed at the sheen of pearls, the taste of spices, and, what concerns us more, at the quantity of textiles of design and weaving unknown to them. These things fascinated the merchants who at once established stores in Palestine and Syria, where they bought from the Mohemmedan the packs of his camels who had journeyed many a weary day over mountain and desert trade routes.

The next move was to fill the transport ships now emptied of Crusading knights with a return cargo of goods from the East, not only from Mesopotamia but from far India and farther Persia and China. Thus the textiles were scattered through Italy of the North. And both designers and weavers took patterns from them.

The Crusades ended in 1270, including even that

pitiful fanatic venture of the Children's Crusade. And it was at this time that the weavers of Italy were busy with the rare material from the silkworm and designers were growing daring knowing that silk would reproduce their drawings in a way impossible to flax or wool.

It is a fantastic story if you wish to dress it up, this influence of the Crusades on trade, but to that can only be attributed a part of the creeping in of Eastern drawing. Constantinople must not be forgotten, once that capital of the Roman Empire, nor Turkey, which captured that same town.

Matters moved slower then than now. A hundred years in textiles saw not the abolition of the Oriental influence so early brought to Italy, but rather its absorption and development.

There is for instance the great motive of the pomegranate and its close relative in design, the Italian artichoke. It began in Persia, and the Mohammedan Empire in adding Persia to its vast possessions, adopted this fine decorative motive. Through Constantinople it came to Italy, and there it altered a trifle because the Italian designer was more familiar with the plant of the artichoke, the leaves of which had shared fame with the acanthus. For perhaps two hundred years the motive was popular with the weavers.

Marco Polo touched Bagdad in the Thirteenth Century, which was then a rich and gorgeous city, and he tells of weaving there, "which included many kinds of silk stuffs and gold brocade wrought with figures of beasts and birds." Mohammedan art had let in Sassanian figures among their arabesques; it was this particular innovation that gave inspiration to weavers in Lucca and Venice.

The Dark Ages were gone. Men were moving about with more freedom, but still the centers of art inclined towards the East, and still men looked to the art of Persia with its romance, Turkey with its flamboyance, Constantinople with its Byzantine convention, and widely to Islam.

The products of these times belong to us now. They are appropriate to our homes. Naturally they are not to be found except in copies, but these copies are expertly made and accompany well the furnishings of a hall of stone walls, a library or dining-room of dark oak. For this reason we like to recall that they represent in design the crystallization of all the romance that went before and the concentrated history of all the peoples who composed the great empires of the Orient.

When Italy came to the fore, Italy as a nation, not as a small part of the Roman Empire, united she was not, but though partitioned under various heads she was recognized as Italy. Roman power—under popes, not emperors—still existed but was limited; Naples was a kingdom with a proper king; Florence was an active democracy, Milan was a center of tyranny under the despots, and Venice as a rich aristocracy stretching a jeweled hand towards the Orient. Here were the materials in which the early Renaissance developed.

And as this awakening reached every department of life, spiritual, intellectual, scientific, industrial, so it was evidenced in the art of weaving, in the art of design and dyeing, and in the employment of silk. Early silks, many from Lucca, show the designs already used in Saracenic art. These make use of the large figures made by a wavy band of ornament enclosing a figure of man or beast or both. The huntsman is the same as the invention of centuries before, and sits his

84

horse while discharging an arrow towards a beast of the forest at his feet.

Another of the early Eastern motives that carried on into the Renaissance was the pair of animals or of birds that face each other or the reverse. Of all the Eastern crystallizations of style that have been unabashed by the passage of centuries, these are the most piquant. They seem to let us into the lives of the people who were brilliant when we were dumb, who were living a life of scientific culture, of art development and of personal indulgence when Europeans were groping in the insensate Dark Ages and content to sleep on straw —glad if the awakening were not a sword-thrust.

The design of the Sassanian huntsman or of his Saracenic copy has about him a youth and eagerness which suggest the noble among the forested mountains in search of sport that he may counteract the ease of the cushioned couch. And the griffins are not without their power to charm, whether they sniff at each other haughtily when vis-à-vis or whether they ignoringly turn away their heads. Their curly tails might belong to mermaids, or they might have been filched from some Chinese carving of low relief done in the times

85

of the Han Dynasty. They were the myths of men who lived so long previous that legend was their only history.

Lions of mad ferocity have their place within spaces circular or ogival, but even more alluring are the birds. These in pairs invariably have their heads reversed. They face each other, breast to breast, and turn away their heads in angry disdain, the hooked beak adding to the general effect of a recent unpleasantness; or their tails are touching, they are back to back, while heads are turned over the shoulder in provocation.

One more favorite animal who traveled in pairs is a lovely beastie that suggests the suave and chivalrous unicorn of two centuries later. He may be a ky-lin of the Chinese, for he has hoofs, he may be a gazelle, for he has the cerf's commanding lift of the head, but he is fitted with a head that conveys idealism in character, and on his body are drawn fantastic lines suggesting wings. It is only in wonderland that such can pasture, it is only from Persian tales that he can have sprung.

The marvelous adaptability of silk made possible the translating of reality and sentiment into the woven fabric. In the early Renaissance when the material be-

86

came plentiful by being produced in Italy, the weavers made lavish and varied use of it. The accompanying essential was design and that was at the time when every man's brush and pencil was busy with ornament. Patterns for artisans were not left to mere pattern-makers to invent, but every artist, no matter how great a painter, applied himself likewise to motives for the liberal arts. Thus, artists were jewelers or marble cutters, or leather illuminators at times.

Velvets of Italy's Sixteenth Century can make of a room a casket for a jewel. They were made on hand-looms with all the patience that entails. The earliest have a pile of generous thread which gives them a depth and richness unsurpassed. It is not alone because these velvets are antiques that collectors prize them but because of their surpassing and peculiar beauty. The touch of the human hand has put magic into them and this is reflected in every fold.

Brocades and damasks poured out of the looms in those prolific times. They were made in Spain as well as in other places, but lest we grow confused it is better to hold ourselves to Italy, the center of the world in the Fourteenth, Fifteenth and Sixteenth Centuries.

87

The Eastern motives of design were giving place to the invention of Italy, yet their fundamental and original impulse can be traced by the savant.

Venice remained long in quasi subjection to the Empire of the East and was also close to the Mohammedan, which explains much in her ·brocades that would otherwise be unintelligible. Besides this she was a seaport of wide importance, dealing with all the nations east of her. Her ships sailed to Constantinople, and to the countries on the eastern shores of the Mediterranean, to which she was the nearest important seaport.

The fabrics brought by the merchants of the Crusades had helped to awaken Europe. They were transported all over Italy—for it was in Italy that the merchants were most active—and found their way into Germany and Central Europe over the Brunner Pass. Thus the culture and art of the East was impressed upon Europe, and here we of European lineage must humbly realize how rude and savage must have been our race while the people of the Orient were rich in art, wise in science, erudite in learning.

Venice was the city which best illustrates the contact

88

with the East, partly because she lay between Europe and the Orient, and was dominated by Constantinople, and partly because of her commerce. She was among the first in Italy to weave in silk, and what more natural than that she should copy the fabrics of the neighboring East. These shortly became involved with motive of European invention, and it is this combination that produced the soft bewitching confusion of design that was peculiarly Venetian even into the Eighteenth Century.

In Florence the Renaissance made its beginnings and developed its earliest notable artists. She had naught to do with merchants and a merchant marine. But she led the northern cities in producing designs of elegance and purity. These were mostly founded on classic motives of that old Roman and Grecian culture that was so worshiped by the creators of the early Renaissance.

The reason for the difference between the ornament of Venice and that of the cities of North Italy is plainly seen, Venice was carrying on the tradition of the Orient while other towns were taking patterns from the Hellenic culture. And these things give

piquancy to the fabrics we handle today when decorating our homes. Each class of design calls loudly
for an appropriate setting. Silks of the Venetian make,
from the earliest up to the late Eighteenth Century,
call for an interior of almost Oriental richness and
would make a clashing contrast in a room of New
England asceticism.

Again, life in Venice was a life of self-indulgence,
of luxury, and early became a life of pageantry. That
amount of colorful public display might also have
drifted in from the Orient. However that may be, the
pageantry of Venice in the Renaissance became one of
the world's sights, and cannot be mentioned even now
without pictures in the mind, pictures of palace bal-
conies hung with rippling brocades, Doges' attendants
arrayed in velvets, gondolas draped with silks and piled
with cushions of silk—all that any Eastern potentate
could have of gold and jewels.

Life in Florence also claimed a share of the increasing luxury. Great men were building magnificent
palaces, the Tornabuoni, the Strozzi, the Medici, different from the rude castles of earlier days, and these
all called for elegant stuffs to soften their stately in-

teriors and make yet more beautiful the famous women of the Renaissance.

The new culture spread at once to the northern towns which began to develop in art, manufacture and commerce notwithstanding the strange rule of the Despots. Milan was ruled over by the Sforza family, one of whom, Ludovico, married Isabella the daughter of the ruling family of Ferrara, the d'Este. Urbino had the only benign overlord, Duke Federigo Gonzaga, so history records, his wife Elizabetta being also a model among women. The Duke established looms within his territory the product of which is still extant.

Although all these tyrannic and powerful gentlemen of the early Renaissance deserved their name of Despots, they nevertheless fostered the arts. They might set apart innumerable persons to die in prison or by the sword, but in matters of cultivation they were eager pupils and almost humble before their instructors. Their children, too, were educated in the classics with a thoroughness unknown to us, and Latin became a familiarly used tongue. To be a murderer and yet a notable patron of the arts was the ambition of every despot. The murdering was a necessity of the time, for a ruler who had snatched his duchy from another by sword and fire must kill at the slightest suspicion any one who might conspire to rob him of his gain and rule in his stead. Notwithstanding all this sanguinary under-current there was much royal entertaining done among the families of the Despots. Most notable were the Venetian visits of Beatrice d'Este and her lady relatives when chests and chests of clothing and hangings were transported thither to make brilliant the occasion.

And at home, in Milan, there were jousts and pageants without number, and so seriously were they taken by Beatrice that she drew the great Michael Angelo away from his immortal works to supply ideas for her gorgeous pageants before the old Castello. Even now, before the old palace of the Sforzas one dreams of these past happenings and the wealth of color displayed by the silken flags and waving brocades of old Milan. Thanks be to the gods that imagination gives the power to roam amid a dull town's utilitarianism and revive a colorful past.

Keep then these three ideas in mind in penetrating the history or the inspiration of woven designs in Italy during the great awakening: the motives of the

Orient, the motives arising from the revival of the classic or Hellenistic and the motives invented or altered by the intelligence of this brilliant period. These last, were they not the spirit of the times using as foundation the already existing motives?

CHAPTER VII

A FEW years ago the Italian Renaissance burst upon an unprepared America that was either English or French in its dictionary of the applied arts. A few erudite and traveled people knew all about the artistic riches of Italy, but even they had no thought of introducing here the beautifying of the private home after the manner of the gifted people of the Renaissance. Principally they brought home from Italian sojourns an angel or two of Fra Angelico, framed in Gothic points of gold, or a few small copies of Della Robbia plaques in glazes of blue and white, placing these exotics amid the Nineteenth Century bibelots.

It was probably Italy's lack of brisk trade among small merchants at home that brought us the Renaissance in furniture and decoration. Thirty years ago, or the early years of the century, the Italian merchant of antiques in Italy languished among his wares, or else took up some occupation and only opened the

94

VENETIAN VELVET, SIXTEENTH CENTURY,
SHOWING THE INTRODUCTION OF THE
CROWN

CRIMSON SATIN BROCADED, GOLD, GREEN, BLUE
BRONSSA, ASIA MINOR SIXTEENTH-SEVENTEENTH CEN-
TURY. CHINESE PEONY DISTORTED IN PLACE OF
POMEGRANATE

shop when sent for by a customer. Americans were the usual buyers in Florence, Rome, Siena, Perugia, Venice. Tens of thousands of Italian immigrants were coming to America—why not send to America the old furniture as well?

It was done, and America received the beauty of the Renaissance into its homes and thrilled with the deep delight of it. Those were the days of the "Collections" much advertised by the auctioneer, the Davanzati, Volpi and many another. They came and came, until most of the old palaces and villas of Italy had lost their splendid treasure of carved wood, gilded and painted panels, forged iron, and treasure chests of textiles.

All these things needed the softening effect of fabrics, and so beautiful were all the velvets, the brocades and tapestries that the intellectual appeal they made could only be gratified by study. And study of the Renaissance leads one directly into a land of romance as fantastic as mythology but as real as history. Our belongings are grown a part of romantic history if we can attach to them a famous name, and it takes but a slight trick of imagination to fancy oneself in intimate association with the former owner and his times. There is not a piece of early fabric that has not its corollary of story about the weave, the material, the design, the use to which the stuff was put, the owner and his history.

When Italy emerged from Medieval necessities into Renaissance luxuries, she constructed villas and palaces which demanded furnishings in keeping. Gothic times had not been times of bodily ease, nor had the furnishing of the homes of great men been anything but scanty. The Renaissance, which embraced every expression of art as well as the growth of intellectual scope, required a new style of furniture for its new style of house. Greece and Rome, being the inspiration for all, the fittings of the house took on designs with the flavor of the classic. Furniture was made after the details of architecture of the ancients. A table was almost a temple with its columnar supports. A chest or cassone was distinctly like an elongated triumphant monument. A credence might be another temple, or at least the portal of a temple. Chairs copied the Roman seat.

Such furniture superb as it was in dignity and in

intellectual value, without hangings and upholstery to soften and decorate it, made of homes mere museums of the cabinet-maker's art. Therefore the weavers were pressed for fabrics of a suitable richness that all this grandeur might be better displayed and that man might be more comforted in his hours of ceremony and of ease.

Translations and paraphrases of architecture, the furniture might be called, and seemed to demand textile designs of large size. Even the silks for costumes were woven in large and elegant patterns as one sees in the costume of Giovanna Tornabuoni painted into the religious fresco of Ghirlandaio.

This was a time when fabrics were lavishly used. Chairs of wooden seats gave way to those softer ones made by stretching a seat canvas over the chair-frame, this to be covered with velvet when not made of leather. In the Seventeenth Century this had grown to a fixed and stuffed upholstery. Backs of chairs no longer of wood were made of a flexible band of canvas stretched from one upright to the other and covered with velvet. When chairs had seats and backs of wood these were fitted with loose cushions—not too thick.

These cushions were finished with galloon and narrow fringe and were tied onto the chair with cord and tassels. This fashion lasted through several centuries even after caning became the mode.

The cassone—that most suggestive article of Italian furniture—was dressed with a flat cover of brocade or velvet or with a thin long cushion. In no case did the cover conceal the work which was lavished on the cassoni by their makers, for this chest was the especial pet of the decorator—the designer being sometimes the architect of the building. It was the uses to which the cassone was put that made it seem worthy of an artist's consideration. It was often the receptacle which held the trousseau of a bride—one of those tenderly young brides of the Renaissance who wrote Latin poems to their fiancés more easily than now one writes a Valentine's Day doggerel. Or, it held the treasure in linen and gold plate which she was bringing her husband as dowry. Once the cassone was a trunk into which to bundle all the Gothic tapestries of a castle when the master went to visit elsewhere or even to make his tent luxurious when he went to war.

The painters of the Renaissance who have decorated

cassoni were among the most celebrated of Italy; the sculptors who carved the wood of cassoni were among those who carved in marble. Thus it is easy to see that a cassone as used today must have as woven decoration nothing which falls below the edge of its flat top.

Eminent architects such as Baccio d'Agnolo and Benedetto da Maiano occupied themselves with some of the furniture designs of the day, for it was the pleasant way of artists in those days not to draw too sharp a line between the fine and the decorative arts, and so the same man played with both. Thus grew the lovely bed of the Fifteenth and Sixteenth Centuries, inviting to repose with its generous space, and lifting the thoughts with the mounting of its beautiful columns or posts, which were carved with the skill lavished on marble details of architecture.

A matter to be always held in mind for the understanding of the draping of the bed is the wretched cold of the houses of the Renaissance. Space, enormous rooms, with ceilings high and windows large, were the rule and gave "the blond assassin Frost" fine opportunity to chill the human anatomy and to pinch until

99

red the pretty noses of the very young beauties whose portraits are left for us to admire.

So the bed with posts and tester or baldaquin was a high favorite, for by drawing close its curtains it could be transformed into a tiny chamber, without draughts and getting gradually warmer from the heat of the sleeper. The top was covered with a lighter stuff, but the side curtains were of the large patterned silks which Italy was then making in her own factories.

In our day we lighten those curtains a bit, as their necessity is gone, and hang scanter lengths or none at all, or perhaps a short flounce around the top. The bed-cover thus takes on greater importance, and in fact is in a far better place to display the richness of old brocade or ancient velvet or their very cleverly made copies of our day. The formation of the bed determines the fashion of the cover. If the sides and foot of the bed are carved or finished to demand display, the cover is merely an oblong to be tucked in and to flow easily over the rolled pillows. One does not think of the bed of the Renaissance as tense with neatness. Its heavy fabrics should have an effect of easy amplitude, thus suggesting the delicious luxury of wrapping the drapery of the couch about one and lying down to pleasant dreams.

If the bed must have its sides covered, then let the cover be extended in simple elegance with none of the flouncings and fripperies of the Eighteenth Century. The wide flat bed on the raised dais looks best with a simple square falling into natural folds at the corners instead of having them shaped or cut. About this bed there is the dignity of a throne, and plain elegance suits it best.

Old pictures of the Renaissance show ever a great simplicity in draping, but the fabrics used reach the highest point in richness. It is to these textiles we turn to reproduce the atmosphere of the golden days of Italy in its highest years. Curtain-hangings—whether for bed or doorway, for window or for background— were merely straight breadths straight-hung. No looping in bunches, nor straining at effects through multiple lines, but all simple. It makes one laugh with glee to see in a Fifteenth Century fresco the use of curtain rings and poles exactly like our own, these on beds or on the wall behind a bed-head.

Elegance was demanded in those times, for the

gratification of the eye more than for actual comfort, it would seem. Wander into the Collegio di Cambio in Siena and look long at the high-backed bench in the entrance. Its marvelous carving in low relief, covering all surfaces but the seat, has served as inspiration to artists for four hundred years and will so continue. Upholstery, textiles are barred by such excess of beauty. What could be added more than a pad of velvet on such a seat, a pad as thin as a biscuit? Its covering must be plain, of a deep and self-effacing color lest it take the eye from the marvelous work of the sculptor in wood. Velvet is preferred, of a blue or green subdued yet distinguished, or of the hazy mauve of aubergine; and tufting is taboo. And this holds good of all benches of the nut-brown wood so loved by the Italians.

Unless the chair of the Renaissance is softened, it makes but an ascetic resting place. Over-stuffed chairs had not been created, but loose cushions were used as lavishly as ease and luxury demanded. They were piled on benches then as now, and tucked behind reclining backs, as well as being placed upon the floor for the greater comfort of those who were short in measure. The *sedia Dantesca*—that chair of little comfort made of crossed supports which must have been inspired by the letter X—was given a cushion on the seat and a softened stretcher in lieu of a back. Add cushions to window-seats as well as to furniture, and you have an array of softeners which may well display the brocades and embroideries of the time.

These homes of the Renaissance with their furnishings of a beauty that can only be called an intellectual product, it is impossible to think of them without falling into delicious reveries about the personalities who lived in those palaces and villas, the great families of Italy. Those kings among merchants, the Medici, how royally they spent the fortune made by their clever commerce. They may have been snubbed a bit at first as being "in trade" and newly sprung from the ranks, but that passed when Lorenzo Medici, the Magnificent, became one of the greatest patrons of art at this time of art's rebirth.

He and his father Cosimo built palaces in the new mode, palaces which abandoned feudal grimness for the finely finished interiors of carved wood-work and frescoed walls, and these he embellished with the fine furniture which reflected the architecture. Then to soften the whole, magnificent velvets and brocades, embroideries and tapestries were used with happy generosity. All the dark brown wood of rooms which might otherwise have been somber, was made glorious by the richness of draperies, covers and cushions, and in such surroundings Lorenzo the Magnificent held court. And his court was not a gathering of thoughtless fashionables of the day; it embraced poets and artists who there found in Lorenzo a generous patron. We cannot think of this great man of the Quattrocento without remembering the exquisite fancies of Sandro Botticelli, whom he kept ever near him and whose frescoes adorned the Medici palace. His exquisite paintings of old Roman myth, Venus, Pallas, Mars, are full of a spirit of fantasy that transports one to Lorenzo's villa at Fiesole, where all art was joyous, and all life was poetry. The lovely Simonetta (*la bella*) so adored by Giuliano Medici and who married at fifteen and died while still but a girl in years, she it was who inspired poets and painters—Botticelli among the rest— as she brightened the life of gay jousts and feasts of the intellect in Florence. Is it irrelevant to mention that one of our merchant-princes, Mr. Gordon Selfridge, acquired the business books of those merchant-princes, the Medici, that he might have them translated for the benefit of all who find romance in the practise of affairs?

Tornabuoni was then a name of prominence, one of them marrying into the family of Medici and becoming the mother of Lorenzo. The sons and daughters of this house also are concerned with the arts of Florence. Giovanna, in her full-length portrait, is arrayed in gorgeous brocaded velvet and is grouped with other women beautifully arrayed.

The name of d'Este is on the lips of all who visit Italy, or of those who study at home. It has magic, the power to bring back the personages of the brilliant years when girls of high birth were women at fifteen and toyed with original verse in Latin as now they toy with "cross-words." Isabella d'Este is called the most charming and brilliant woman of the Renaissance, though that is a statement where perhaps the use of the superlative may provoke the mention of a score of other names.

These women of the Renaissance seem to have had an intelligence—and intellect—far surpassing that of folk we know today. They were learned beyond our standard, they were able in emergencies to seize the reins of government and reign wisely in the place of dead or absent husbands, they managed with thrift their large establishments, they attended jousts and pageants where they were the toast of all, they fostered art in its various expressions, nor hesitated to ask artists of the highest rank to make for them the furniture of their rooms, to design the brocades for hangings or dresses.

In Mantua—still in the Fourteen Hundreds—the Gonzagas ruled, for North Italy was not then a united country but was a group of petty states each governed by dukes and despots. And it was to Mantua that womankind turned for the fashions in textiles and the manner of using them. The name of a dressmaker became a Mantua-maker, and that name was in use even in mid-Victorian times as all can see who read Dickens. Even the women of France turned to the Gonzaga's town of Mantua for their modes instead of to Paris, in the Fifteenth Century.

And so through all the Fifteenth and Sixteenth Centuries in Italy, the lovely ladies of wit and beauty loved and sang, were exquisite in the way that Botticelli portrays them or serious with responsibility as Ambrogio de Predis paints them, and it is of these almost mythical beings that one dreams when left alone in a room which happily cheats one with its charm of ancient days.

And the men of those times—why do I not speak of the brilliant princes? Because ever and always the human habitation is made for woman, made to shelter her, embellished to delight her. And man stands by and glows with satisfaction at his work and with delight in her for whom it was executed.

Italy's Renaissance was founded on the old culture of Greece and Rome. Its first stirrings were a matter of the intellect. The original manuscripts of the old writers were unearthed and studied. Every one of education learned Greek that he might translate the drama, and Latin that he might know the poets. This was not the time when man could scan the backs of his several editions and pick his book. There were no books. An ambitious Medici set two hundred men at copying to make him a library. At the end of two years' close labor they delivered to him forty-five volumes—and that is no more than one gets at Christmas nowadays.

The men of the early awakening then went to the ancient manuscripts of the classics, and on these the new culture was formed. It was the new growth of a vigorous and intelligent people grafted on the old tree of Greek and Roman ideals. Soon the spirit of the invigorated classics was expressed in art, in design, in ornament. But the development was Italian and Italian only. After Italy had produced this prodigious revival, other countries—one after the other—took pattern from her, copied her, in other words. France, under Henri II, began to alter her designs and Francis I deliberately brought Italians to his court to practise their art for his palaces and châteaux. Henry VIII of England did the same. And thus the Renaissance traveled, but only in Italy did it properly develop. In all other countries it was imported, not inherent. And as all the world of Rome's time followed Hellenic ideals, so all the world of the Fifteenth and Sixteenth Centuries followed Italy's.

CHAPTER VIII

THE FRENCH NATIONAL STYLE

WE are now in the time of Louis XIV. That Grand Monarch, as he liked to be called, was a liberal patron of the arts. But art patrons after the decline of the Renaissance wanted display, not thought, so designs grew prodigious. Delicate drawings which so pleased the intelligent ladies of Florence, Milan, Ferrara, failed to express the spirit of the Seventeenth Century, therefore the mode changed. France was creating a style of decoration all her own. If it was more grandiose and sumptuous than intellectual, that should be overlooked because it was at least a new creation in the world of decoration, and it built a foundation for the styles that followed those of the Eighteenth Century.

Louis XIV in his maturity is a pompous and powerful figure, but in his youth he excites our interest and wonder as an individual. He was but five years old when his father's death left him to reign. That in itself is full of appeal and invests the heart with a tenderness for him—a useless waste, for he was ever able to fend for himself.

His mother, the beautiful Anne of Austria, with the astute Cardinal Mazarin, gave him his early training. Mazarin had the Italian's love for art and its true appreciation. The royal boy was early associated with the works of art of the Cardinal and learned from him his connoisseurship. We are not without at least one of the textile examples of the Mazarin collection, the rare old tapestry made for Ferdinand and Isabella and now in the collection of Mr. Joseph Widener of Philadelphia.

Foucquet had long been Minister of State when Louis began to govern. One of his greatest interests had been to acquire for himself a colossal fortune. After the showy manner of the day he displayed his wealth in Paris and in his marvelous château and gardens at Vaux. Lively ladies made beautiful the garden shades, gallant gentlemen in beauteous dress accompanied them, and the heart of Nicolas Foucquet warmed with pride. But the king although young in years suspected him of touching the coffers of

PERSIAN SILK DEPICTING A HUNT. SIXTEENTH CENTURY

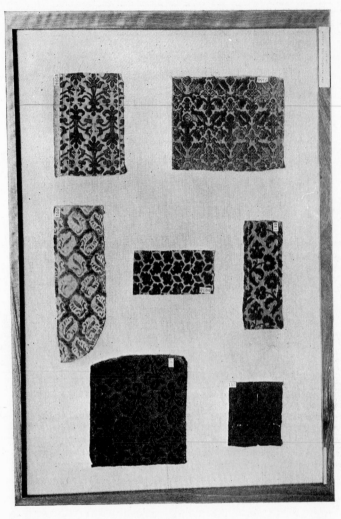

ITALIAN VELVETS. SIXTEENTH-SEVENTEENTH CENTURIES. THESE SMALL PATTERNS IMMEDIATELY FOLLOWED THE LARGE DESIGNS

France for his fortune and without hesitation had him arrested. He died after nearly twenty miserable years of imprisonment.

And thus came Colbert to the fore, and the subject of our study is somewhat concerned with this able Minister of Finance. If the king, Louis XIV, was by early training a lover of art, it was because of the wise administration of State affairs by Colbert that Louis was able to create an actual manufactory for art, maintained by the Treasury of France.

The inspiration was found, as it ever is, among social conditions. First there were the ladies of the Court, beautiful like Louise de Vallière, gifted like Madame de Montespan. For these and many others, including perhaps the Queen, Louis desired a sumptuous setting, furniture and hangings that should make appropriate background for hours of ease and intimacy. And for royal audiences, there were required things even more grandiose.

Again there were the artists. Louis XIV seemed to have in his hard ambitious nature a tenderness towards artists. They were ever a badly recompensed portion of society—with the notable exception of a flatterer in portraits—and one thinks of them as running around the Place des Voges or older streets with canvasses to sell, and of returning unsuccessful to attic chambers in the high houses of old Paris. But the king rewarded them with free quarters in the Louvre.

Louis XIV founded the Manufacture des Gobelins, and Colbert furnished the money to maintain it. Here were made the most marvelous pieces of furniture of the time, bringing into prominence such names as Riesner, Oeben, Caffieri. And in this factory we come upon the revival of tapestry weaving.

Each part of the world has its day in art. Art seems too precious and rare a matter to spread over all the world at once, so it blesses one country at a time. The valley of the Euphrates and Egypt had their day, Greece had hers, followed by Rome. Then the Mohammedan dominated. Italy awoke and aroused a lethargic civilization. Next and last to impress the entire world was France. The French Renaissance, the period is called by some, but that term not being exact turns one back to the time when Francis I imported the Italian Renaissance into his country with the enthusiasm of the true lover of beauty.

The flowering of France during the Eighteenth Century could not have occurred without preparation, and that preparation was made under the hand of Louis XIV.

It was a part of the monarch's policy and pleasure to spend vast sums on luxury. Finding no palace in Paris adequate for his pomps and ceremonies he built the palace of Versailles and laid out the adjoining city for those courtiers who should require to be near.

Peculiar and tyrannic were his methods of getting the money for such an indulgence. He extracted it from the State Treasury without asking leave, and commanded the services of peasants and military folk without pay. With great forethought for his personal indulgence he retained for himself the place of prime minister. His father, Louis XIII, had been dominated by Cardinal Richelieu, but Louis XIV rejected the example, calling his father a weakling. So with no one to stay his hand, he proceeded majestically on his pompous way.

The place of this king in France was almost that of a god. By royal decree Louis made the people feel that he and God were one; to disobey one was to offend the Other. To impart such an idea to a nation was an act of genius.

Kings are out of fashion now, and we make merry today over the prodigious wigs of Louis XIV, over the short monarch's four-inch heels, and his lack of humor which kept him ever cognizant of his own greatness— but the more serious facts of history justify his title of the Grand Monarch and the self-importance which led him to take the blazing sun as his personal emblem.

He was the first French king with complete power. The nobles of France had been at times controllers of their king. Entrenched in their fortified castles they had dared to differ with royal decrees. But now the castle was giving way to the château, and the fighting nobles became courtiers at Versailles.

The magnificence of pomp and ceremony at the Court was the admiration and envy of the courtiers. Wars were continued, however, and the king was ever ready to indulge in their expense of blood and gold. But through it all Louis impressed on his people his own dominant idea that kings were God-given, that they should be obeyed as the agent of God, that criticism was iniquitous.

But there was another side of a king's life, the private and more intimate life of contacts with those who came close to him. Versailles was a place where courtiers flocked, where those who had something to impart or to gain were able to reach the king, and thus came the habit of receiving in the royal bedroom when a privileged guest might hand the monarch his shoes, another might adjust his wig.

And these visitors found themselves among the most magnificent surroundings. The royal bed rivaled the throne in design and in wealth of draping. It stood upon a dais; it was sheltered with a canopy of carved and gilded wood from which depended curtains long and full, of the most gorgeous brocade or damask. The windows were hung with the same, and armchairs were for the first time stuffed firmly on their frame instead of being fitted with the capricious loose cushion of former years. Hangings on the walls which in winter were used to soften the asperities of the weather, flowed loose from the walls as hangings should ever do. The Gobelins factory and the city of Lyons was producing these luxuries for the monarch's use.

In the midst of all the royal elegance and pomp, one

sees the figures of the court ladies, whether at great functions or in the more intimate hours. This was a time when volume was the mode in dress as in draperies. With characteristic imperiousness the king forbade the wearing of gold brocade to all but royalty and favorites. However much the king might emphasize the value of pure living, we know that he was dominated by certain ladies who have become historic —the queen was not among them—and their lives are ever of interest. But how the king had time for sweet dalliance with ladies is difficult of understanding. He worked ardently for almost all of his waking hours. The life of a great monarch who also is his own prime minister includes little time for play.

Louis XIV is said to have had four hundred beds, but that might easily be if they were sprinkled through his various palaces and lodges. So important was the bed that picturesque names were given it. The *lit de parade* was the most elegant of all. It was covered with the square canopy of carving from which the heavy curtains hung, sometimes capped with a line of embroidered tabs. And its coverlid and pillows of silken stuffs gave to it the elegance of a throne. It

stood on a dais, beyond which the ministers and no-
bles might stand when the king gave an audience.
Princes of the blood might sit upon the bed or near it.
All others save these two classes knelt upon the floor.
In this imposing setting the king conserved his strength
by reclining during audiences.

It is the fashion to criticize the taste of Louis XIV
in styles of decoration, but it should never be forgot
that they are an expression of the reign, and they were
the foundation of the more exquisite styles immediately
following. Louis XIV had big work to do in enlarg-
ing France, in uniting her, in reaching out to increase
her possessions. Only a man of extreme self-assurance
and self-concentration could so well have advanced the
national unification. Understanding his pride and self-
importance the artists of the time composed for him a
decoration which shouted aloud that Louis XIV was
the greatest of living men. They were such able men
as Mansart, Le Brun, Le Pautre, Boulle, and together
they made a style of magnificence and homogeneity,
an expression of the nation.

Louis during middle life paraded around the palace
of Versailles rejoicing in the visible evidence of his

greatness, but when he grew old the weight of magnificence oppressed him and he asked of his artists that they infuse into their works some of the spirit of childhood. And on this was founded the lightening of style that was developed in the Regency and in the next two reigns. The incomparable Watteau was of the last years of Louis XIV.

Colbert stands side by side with the king until the former's death in 1683. He it was who ever found the money for the king's extravagance and for the nation's progress. The Revocation of the Edict of Nantes cost France fifty thousand of able workers, but Colbert brought up the production of textiles by the simple expedient of prohibiting the importation of any foreign stuffs. We can see in that a reason for the concentration on French products that brought about the flowering of the styles of "the Louis'."

In the reign of Louis XIV enormous amounts of woven stuffs were consumed. They added to the sumptuousness of all rooms when hung in voluminous folds and draped in deep festoons. The entire wall was sometimes loosely hung with silk, or only certain sections of a room. Doorways were hung, and win-

dows, both with a heaviness that we cannot well imitate in the conditions of modern living.

The bedstead had but little ornamentation, it being
the fashion to conceal all wood-work with the drapery.
In fact the draping of the state bed or most important
bed in the house involved enormous expense. There
was the canopy or tester upheld by posts, the canopy
à la duchesse which was supported only from the
wall, the dome bed and many other variants all demanding curtains, lambrequins, coverlets. A drapery
of tapestry or embroidery which differed from the bed
curtains was hung on the wall at the bed's head. This
might be the sole piece of its kind in the bed's draping and handsomer than all the rest. In the bed *à la
duchesse* it frequently matched the coverlet which
swept from pillow to floor the entire length of the bed,
there being no posts to interfere, nor any curtains, save
those at the head to keep light from the sleeper's eyes.

Six full curtains supplied the bed of four posts, entirely hiding them. Until late in the Seventeenth Century the state bedroom was used also as a dining room
by persons of the upper middle class, merchants who
lived with a certain elegance. This accounts for the

amplitude of curtains which made it possible to shut up the bed entirely so that it stood like an armoire or other impersonal piece of furniture. It eliminated all suggestions of use and looked overpoweringly architectural. Other days, other ways, is our comment.

One thinks always of silken stuffs as draping the beds of the time, brocades, velvets, damasks. But records show that woolen textiles also were in great favor. A peculiarly elegant woolen material was called camelot, and this was preferred in white. Red cloth was also in vogue, and we can fancy it imported from both Flemish looms and English. An old description of a bed mentions the curtains as olive cloth lined with changeable taffeta in red and blue, with trimmings and fringe, a wall hanging of tapestry at the head. It is Molière who writes of this bed and dresses it up still further with an old rose canopy of fine serge.

Crimson was the favorite color of the time. We find here a certain expression of the reign. Pale blue and sea-shell pink would have ill-expressed the spirit of the reign of Louis XIV.

In windows we find a novelty during the period, the amazing innovation of window curtains split up the middle and drawn to both sides instead of being drawn to one side only. Again the modern has to laugh at the small stupidities in customs of the past. Late in the Seventeenth Century muslins and prints arrived from India. They were at once adopted for bedrooms.

Of chairs there is not much to recall that is inappropriate for today. The manner of upholstery is modern. Earlier chair cushions were removable, indeed the cushions of a room were ever carried from piece to piece of furniture to ease an aching back or add to the luxury of a sybarite. And later, in the Eighteenth Century, the squab cushion was familiar on the seats of upholstered chairs. But the square, balanced chair of Louis XIV was fitted with permanent upholstery. The fault in the modern copy lies often in over-stuffing the back which should be flat.

It was in these generous elegant chairs, covered with richest brocaded velvet that *les précieuses*—the fops of Molière's time—disposed their persons in elegant attitude and meticulous manner.

The sense of dignity in the style named for Louis XIV had begun to alter before his death in 1715. The newer lighter mode seemed to presage the lighter spirit in living that the Regent introduced and that continued until the Revolution. Madame de Maintenon being in the anomalous position of wife but not queen removed her influence, and the more frivolous characters had their way.

CHAPTER IX

DEVELOPMENT UNDER LOUIS XV

WHEN the mind dwells on the styles that are truly French, it is always in Versailles that they have their locale. Louis XIV built the palace, but it was also the setting for the succeeding reigns and styles. As all know, the king arbitrarily settled on a marshy tract as the place where Versailles was to be built, Mansart drawing the plans and pressing the work with great loss of life among the fever-stricken workers. But to make life intimate and gracious within the great spaces of the palace was scarcely possible. It spoke of pomp and ceremony only. Even Louis XIV built a smaller palace in maturity where he and Madame de Maintenon might retire to an approximation of home life—the Trianon.

It was perhaps in the out-of-doors that life was most enjoyed in the time of Louis XIV, and that is the life depicted in the ornament of his day. The palace grounds included flower beds and fountains, bosquets of green shade and leafy privacy. Le Nôtre was the artist who advised, and he provided both the pompous and the secluded. The gardens included the magnificent series of terraces we see today, descending in fountains and groves to the lakes, but to right and left all through the forest he planted enchanting apartments of living green, decorating these leafy chambers with statuary or with slight architectural effects—"gardens in which art improves upon nature," Ninon de Lenclos had said.

The decorators of Louis XV seized at once on these beautiful conceits as background for playful scenes, and set within them the ladies in their elegance with much silken drapery, and the gay gallants with their apparel no less gorgeous except in volume. *Fêtes champêtres* became the diversion of the day and these picnics of the court gave inspiration to Watteau and Pater and a train of followers. The contrast of voluminous silken brocades in rich coloring displayed in the informality of the out-of-doors, was irresistibly piquant. Added to this was the charm of playful youth and the witchery of the greenwood, the surrounding forest. The very trees prompted gay mischief, and so we have

124

the decorative scenes of men and maids playing at love and playing at sports. Artificiality had its part in all these games, as when it became the fashion to play at being haymakers, gardeners and the like; but it is supposable that when a crowd of very young and utterly idle people are turned out from the formal palace into limitless forest and gardens, their play becomes both genuine and reckless.

The gardens of Versailles not only furnished these scenes of *fêtes galantes* and *fêtes champêtres* but marvelous water parties under the full moon, with music adding to the witchery, and boats filled with the lively persons of the court, pelting other boats with roses and assailing ears with daring provocations from safe distance. All these alluring pictures were put on canvas by the masters of art, to the delight of beauty lovers then and now.

But the gardens inspired also those who drew designs for the associated arts. There grew the marvelous flowers that were taken as designs for the silks being woven at Lyons for the costumes and decorations of the day.

It was a hundred and fifty years earlier in the day

of the patriotic Henri IV, the father of his people, that France had her first great public garden for the cultivation of flowers. This king obtained a wide tract of land and devoted it to advancing horticulture. When sufficiently equipped with the best flowers of France, under capable gardeners, this place was named *le Jardin du Roi,* but the king devoted it to the interest of the people. Here artists were invited to come to study the plants that they might make original designs. Thus began a greater originality in floral ornament, which replaced a copying of the Italian Renaissance.

The enormous difference between the earlier types of flower and leaf, those woven in the silks of Louis XIV, and those of his successor is due to the fact that the artists were at the earlier date still under the spell of a formal composition. Even though they drew their designs from the flowers of the king's garden, or any garden of France, they arranged them with a precision which kept them unnatural. Perfect balance in a set design, and a building up of full flower and leaf into enormous display was the dominating idea. Because of the absence of shading all designs were flat.

CHINESE DAMASK OF EIGHTEENTH CENTURY, CON-
VENTIONALIZED PEONY WITH SCROLLS

CHINESE VELVET, CUT AND UNCUT, LOTUS AND
LEAF SCROLLS, EIGHTEENTH CENTURY

Was it the life of the court beauties among the greenery and the flowers of the gardens that freed the artist from convention? It seems so. Whereas the spirit of the court was majestic and conventional under Louis le Grand, the spirit of the court was gay and free under Louis le Bien-aimé. And it is exactly this difference that is expressed in the textiles of the two eras. Louis XIV brocades amaze us with a recognizable command; Louis XV brocades thrill us with delight, and unite us in sympathy to the people of that past so rich in beauty.

The big rose of the Louis XV brocade bending heavy on its stem, sparkling with metal threads, is it not the same as that with which a daring Phyllis tapped the ear of Strephon as he stepped through the dew-silvered gardens? And the sprays of big blue hyacinths, were they not gathered at the edge of the wood where a mock Diana received them from a laughing Acteon? They liked to play at the classics in the Eighteenth Century, and if you assumed a name for play's sake you might consistently carry out the part and get no shame for it, the blame being on the gods not on those who took their names.

The gardens of Versailles and elsewhere gave not only flowers to the artists to play with, but the bits of architecture near which they grew. The flowers were no less sophisticated than the gardens, and so took well their association with a balustrade, a pedestal, or some such marble accompaniment. They were lush, voluptuous flowers, full of vitality, of color, and also suggesting graceful freedom of movement under the garden's caressing zephyrs. Always they hinted at something beyond vegetation, something human.

There was much to express in those days. The spirit of the times if thoroughly delineated would express two opposing forces, the extravagant indulgences of court and aristocracy, and the even stronger determination of thinking people to attain liberty. The Revolution was approaching, but art told little of its coming. Louis XV the king was the first in the world to be pleased, for he had an unlimited treasure with which to employ artists, and how could they satisfy him better than by depicting the joys with which he filled his time?

As for his character we all know he came to the throne too young, that he married at sixteen the Polish

Princess Marie Leczinska seven years older than he, that he was shy, dull and proper in marital behavior, and that his queen was occupied for the first ten years of marriage in giving him ten children. They settled into some of the smaller rooms at Versailles where the king could live more informally.

Then came Madame de Pompadour, followed by Madame du Barry. To these two women must we attribute much of the marvelous flowering of Eighteenth Century art—art meaning all arts. The part these women played was not that of creator, but of art patron—with the coffers of the crown as counting-house. But thereby hangs a tale as interesting as any in the history of kings. What the king himself lacked in initiative, in ambition, in art appreciation, these two women supplied. Had the king been more efficient, less bored with life, the exquisite art with which his reign was distinguished might have been attributed to him, but it was really based on the wish of the artists to please the taste of the king's famous mistresses.

Into this art crept not only great beauty but also the signs of the times, the events of history, which afforded inspiration and were thus recorded. For example, France—not the king—was turning her attention towards the East. That great maker of nations, the merchant marine, of England, of Holland, of France had been for some time securing coast cities in Asia and even annexing territory. The Dutch had possessed themselves of Java and the Moluccas, once called the Isles of Spice, and England starting with Madras, laid claim to the government of India, while France had taken Pondicherry.

France, on looking about for more territory she could claim without resort to war with these strong nations, remembered the peninsula of Indo-China. There she had planted her flag, at Tourane, a tiny port of Annam. Tonkin adjoined it, and China lay just beyond. Gay little sorties took place, the Annamites being haughtily surprised at those who dared intrude on their heritage of seclusion, the French being equally surprised at the resistance of the unreadable enemy to the army of a great European power. Officers reveling at late banquets were slaughtered and all sorts of unpleasant unexpecteds happened. But finally the conflict was over, and French ships sailed home trailing after them, so to speak, the little countries that compose most of Indo-China.

And the effect on the decorative arts in France was amazing. An entirely new alphabet of design grew from this importing of motives from Tonkin and Annam. Superficially thinking one attributes it to China. But great China with its ancient art and culture had she given the fundamentals of her art, would have infused a quite different spirit into French artists. Indeed Chinese art could not in its grandeur have been absorbed by the then pervading spirit of France.

But the art of Tonkin and Annam where the French flag was planted, was an adaptation of Chinese art by a neighbor far behind in seriousness and development. This art takes all its motives from the Chinese, but makes them miniature and exquisite, developing craftsmanship to an almost unbelievable perfection, but omitting great motives of profound thought.

Thus the art taken home by the victorious French was one of preciosity, of lightness. Withal it was exotic, and into this the French injected gaiety. Also they stopped not at the designs themselves but pictured with them the natural life of the Eastern land—as they saw it, not as it really was. To them the Asiatic was a humorous being almost on the plane with an amusing monkey, and the artists so depicted him, perched gaily among airy curves often in combination with that same monkey. He was above all fantastic and adapted to the light touch in decoration.

The supposed Chinese habitat, too, appeared in design, especially for weaving into silk, and thus we have a series of charming little bridges, of tiny pagodas and of temples. The latter were innocently taken for houses by the designers who never having seen the usual Indo-Chinese home of bamboo poles and thatch, were unhampered by the inelegant truth. Thus we have the base of the bewitching designs called Chinoiserie, the invention of the artist multiplying details and treating all with lightness and charm.

The conspicuous invention in ornament in the style named for Louis XV was the combining of the varied irregular curve in a way to produce perfect balance. These irregular curves—does not one see in them a Chinese motive? Has not the outline of the Chinese bat very much to do with these curves. The bat of the Chinese as used in weaving is a very different design from ours. He is caught when wheeling, and dodging, not with evenly extended wings, making curves, not angles.

The factories of Lyons were not slow to produce silks after these novel patterns.

The stories of Mesdames de Pompadour and du Barry have been told so many times that I hesitate to tell them here, so merely recall the side of their lives that bears upon our subject. That the king himself was not worthy of the position of king, placed all the greater influence in the hands of those surrounding him. One could not fancy Louis XIV allowing a courtesan to rule.

The French Royal Academy of Arts formed by Colbert with Louis XIV was still operative, and the Manufacture des Gobelins. With such resources at hand almost anything could be created at command. Gathered near these were such able artists as Boucher, Lancret, Fragonard, with their delicious canvases, and Huet, Oudry, Van Loo, with their inexhaustible invention of design. To these we turn for the beauty of the style. Louis XV being but a child when taking

133

the throne, the Regent Philippe d'Orléans had eight years in which to play with the newly attempted curves, and then occurred perhaps the loveliest moment of the style named for the king himself.

Perhaps it was the reign of La Pompadour which overdeveloped the style, for it is ever true that character expresses itself in design. This remarkable woman is either an accomplished courtesan or a minister of state, according to the part of her life one studies. The early pictures of her are poignant and bewitching. When very young her determination to charm the king led her to place herself within range of his vision in startling novelty, that he might become aware of her existence. He met the beauty in the forest driving a pair of dashing horses while seated alone in a carriage like the shell of Venus. And every day she passed before him as he went to hunt, and always she appeared in a new and amazing dress and carriage. She won the royal lover, of course, and many books recount her life with its wanton pleasures, its licentiousness, its mad extravagance. But there was another Pompadour, a woman of force, of many gifts, of appreciation of art, and of great ability in the world of

134

politics, of government. Without this strength she would have passed as many another king's mistress has passed, leaving a trace of interest only to those who like to peep into cupboards where naughty secrets lie hid.

We of today owe tribute to La Pompadour for the encouragement she gave to all the decorative arts. The manufactory of the crown supplied for her and for the king the most beautiful furniture that France has produced, including all the *orfèvrerie* or gilt bronze ornament that accompanied it, as well as pretty trifles without number.

Lyons was feverishly busy in those days. The king was not satisfied to limit his living to the palace at Versailles, but built houses in the town and outside of it for his beautiful companion. The present Hotel des Reservoirs, giving on the Park, was one of these. All the new domiciles required silks to drape their windows and beds and to cover their chairs, and Lyons must supply them as better weaving was done there than even in Italy. We have a perfect reflection of the designs of the day in the patterns of the silk of Lyons.

As the reign grew older there was the tendency to

throw onto the surface of the silk some of the fripperies of feminine fashions. Thus came the fancy of weaving a pattern of undulating ribbons and lace straying across a brocade, twisted here and there with a floral chain, and crossed at intervals with a stem of realistic flowers. It recalls the ancient silks where bands of ornament formed ogival shapes, but shows the world to be another planet in its new expression.

Lace shared place in these new designs with plumes and feathers. Consult the portraits of the times and see the enormous quantity of trimmings which went to ornament a woman's toilettes, and find therein the reasons why the designers drew them for the weavers. Yet after all they have not half the lusciousness of those earlier silks of the style where flowers alone supplied the motive and metal threads gave effect of sunbeams and moonshine, of dew and glistening water.

Just as the dresses were rich and voluminous, so were the draperies of the house. We never weary of making the comparison, for it reveals a harmony of thought. Both dress and drapery of the home are composed for women. Then is it not reasonable that a similarity should exist between the two at a given era?

136

The time came when walls were no longer hung with full drapings of silk. The wood carvers in the Royal factories were having their day. Not only were they carving furniture with their clever hands, but they had seized the wide spaces of the walls as well, to ornament. Thus arose the fashion of wood-work for which we like to retain the French name of *boiserie*. In its most monopolizing mode it covers all the walls, but often large panels are left, and these were filled with silk mounted on muslin and tacked firmly behind the wooden molding. Note what a difference in expression this gives a room, what prettiness of formality.

Curtains for the window and for the bed grew laughably like the costumes of ladies at the court of Versailles. The silks of which they are made are the same, both in coloring and design. As the skirt was voluminous so were the draperies. Lavish expenditure was the order of the day, the king and La Pompadour setting the example, so the appalling expense of the toilettes affrighted no one.

As skirts were many yards around, it was desirable to ornament their vast spaces, so there came drapings edged with fringe, ribbons sewn on in waves, lace the same. And all these things were copied in the curtains. A window might no longer be hung with a simple breadth, it must show as many complications as the ladies' frocks. And so came lambrequins, and curtains that fell but a little way before their fulness was caught up that it might fall again. The lambrequin was made of ample lengths, several of them, and these were draped one over the other with the avoidance of repeated curves which makes the charm of the rococo. And of course no other people than the French could play on this same rococo theme without falling from good taste.

The bed was inclining to loose the heavy canopy and to lower the posts. We can almost see there the touch of La Pompadour. A becoming setting for a woman reclining in bed was of first import when women received in bed. And however much it might have suited Marie de' Medici to be half-obliterated by black velvet curtains, La Pompadour would prefer to lie in plain view, a fresh-plucked rose on a silken cushion.

Not that canopy and curtain had disappeared, but

the other mode existed with it, just as it does today. The canopy followed the fashion of complex festoons with trimmings, but more tasteful were draperies of silk that by the richness of the fabric fell in swelling line and were artistically held by the posts at head and foot of the bed.

It was when the posts were gone that the most charming effects were gained. The canopy became then but a small semi-circle of gold from which depended silken stuffs distending themselves in clouds such as those that cupids loved, the rosy playful cupids of the Eighteenth Century which seemed to retain something of the infantile in spite of the sophisticated life they shared.

Such a drapery made a nest of tinted shadows around the pillows and over the face of her who reposed thereon. Add to it a coverlet of the same silks and the resting place of woman has reached its perfection of beauty. The bed was sometimes placed against the wall, and then its ends must be alike, the canopy placed in the middle with its pendent curtains flowing to right and to left over head and foot; or the bed was slipped within a niche too small to be called an alcove, and from this hung the draperies, long ones to secure privacy or warmth, and shorter ones to make a complicated lambrequin. And these are the styles that we are still carrying today.

A word about the bed-cover. In the beginning of the Louis XV period it followed the fashion of being a large flat square or oblong, split for the accommodation of bed posts at the foot, and drawn up over the pillows at the head. Later it was furnished with a flounce, all in accord with the bouffant toilettes of the ladies of the day.

This flounce was set on with galloon and was not a simple flounce at all, but had a double box-plait to contain the amplitude as well as the full gathers. Both devices were needed to dispose prettily of the mass of silk. Taffeta was the silk most liked for all bed-draperies in the second half of the Eighteenth Century as it best carried out the ideas in vogue of cloud-like lightness.

CHAPTER X

IF the styles of Louis XV expressed exquisitely the
voluptuousness of the court, to the period is also
attributable a return to the purity of the classic. And
here too we must look to the dominating personages
of the court to find reasons for a new stiffening of
lines, a correction of too much that was curved, too
little that was simple.

For Madame de Pompadour was made the style
called Louis XV that caused France to be imitated all
over the world. Throughout the history of modern
design in Europe none other has reached its originality.
Perhaps it was the only one that was an absolute creation and not a copying of imported design.

An element that contributed to the perfection of the
style was the willingness of the king to pay enormous
sums to artists and artisans to relieve them from all
financial worries, leaving their minds free for creation
and the exercise of skill. The manufacture of all the

articles that contribute to the ornament of a house had never before or since been relieved of the necessity of profit. The Royal Manufactory instituted by Colbert was continued by Louis XV and his successor.

Only the extraordinary personal power of kings could have produced such liberal spending. Conflicts between a king and his nobles had ceased, warrior lords had gradually changed from jealous rivals of the monarch into courtiers at Versailles seeking for the king's favor at fêtes and levees. The common people and the bourgeois were taxed beyond their endurance, and thus came the money which supplied the coffers of the king. And this was the money spent on La Pompadour and the artistic creations for her numerous residences.

When revolt of the people came, an indignant searcher after detail counted the sums spent for the king's great mistress and found she had cost France millions of livres. But it was more than that. She was one of those who were bringing on the Revolution. She was the glaring exponent of the weakness of kings. Richelieu had ably built up the idea of a king's unassailable power and divinity. Madame de

PERUVIAN TAPESTRY WEAVE, PRE-INCA, COASTAL
REGION, OF CHIMU CULTURE

Pompadour after a hundred years was showing the people how false, licentious and oppressive a king could be.

And thus came the Encyclopedists with Diderot at their head, men of intellect who could scorn a king and his follies and who held the eternal verities as higher than a monarch. And by gradual filtration of ideas throughout the nation, the people of France questioned things; they questioned the right of Louis to over-tax the humbler classes that he might empty the money into the lap of an outrageous woman whose *métier* was only to amuse and tyrannize.

Thus came the demand for a change, and there followed the Revolution, which never was intended to be a bath of blood, but only a re-adjustment, a restoration of justice. But we are reaching ahead of the story. It is difficult not to do so in any Eighteenth Century review, for one reign runs into another in matters artistic. La Pompadour was finished. Madame du Barry, far younger, replaced her and was at the Court of Versailles when the king died—of small-pox, that loathsome disease which was so prevalent in France at that time.

But before this a new element had come into the Royal Household. The Dauphin had taken a wife, the exquisite Austrian princess Marie Antoinette. This was in 1770, four years before the death of Louis XV.

It was but natural that such an event as the entrance of Marie Antoinette should inspire the artists of the day. It gave a new spirit to design, new motives. Looking back we cannot say that originality was rampant, as in the heyday of La Pompadour, but at least a simplicity appeared to prune the curving rococo before it began to slip into the decadence that ruins all over-growths.

The style named for Louis XVI has its base in the classic lines of Greece. Two reasons governed the creating artists. One was the correctness and purity of the young Dauphiness Marie Antoinette, whose character they wished to indicate and whose taste they wished to please; the other was the newly excavated Pompeii, which was furnishing a new Greco-Roman inspiration to artists in all countries, but especially in France.

All classes of design underwent a change. Note the difference between the floral silks called Louis XV and

144

those named for Marie Antoinette. Both are equally
naturalistic in treatment, but a striking difference is in
their reactions given to the beholder. The one brings
visions of a lush vegetation associated with a sensual
humanity, as when a heavy-headed crimson rose curves
over the golden surface of a rich brocade. The other
shows the little flowers, the darlings of the wood and
fields, thrown sparsely on pale taffeta, turning one's
thoughts to simpler delights.

Marie Antoinette was the daughter of that notable
mother, Marie Thérèse of Austria and Hungary, who
had trained her daughter in all the virtues. Louis XV
died four years after the marriage and his grandson
came to the throne as Louis XVI. This made of
the Dauphiness a queen, and for her were named
many of the inventions of the day in a decorative
way.

Louis XVI was in character just the man wanted as
argument against the power of kings. Parallel with
the life of court and courtier ran the life of the intellectuals who were in rebellion against the injustices
committed by the crown. These latter looked upon
those products of art which the Royal Manufactories

had been so prodigally producing, as souvenirs of an elegant immorality.

Voltaire was calling for free speech. He who had flattered and humored La Pompadour at court now announced himself the friend of the merchant class, declaring he liked them far better than the aristocrat. And all France was becoming educated to a new and radical thought. Louis XVI was scarcely the man to note the signs of the times or to meet political emergencies.

His was a little mind, pleased with little things, his workshop, his weaving, his gardening. And the beautiful queen also had none of the power of a leader. They therefore lived at Versailles in the midst of the Courtiers with eyes closed to all except to playing the Ancient Régime.

A taste grew for the miniature; the Petit Trianon was built for the king and queen to use as a grown-up's playhouse. The queen liked to play at dairy-maid, and had a small equipment assembled to favor the fancy, *le Hameau*. Small rooms were preferred to large, and the classic flavor of Pompeian motives dominated the *boiserie*. Tapestries grew small, were no longer ample hangings, but shrank to pettiness and were used only to fill small panels or to cover furniture.

Silks suffered also, yet because of a certain preciosity in design they are dear to us now in this day of eclectic taste. They lost their magnificence but they gained in charm. The great flower designs built up of large flower upon larger flower, the brocades of naturalistic flowers from highly cultivated gardens, gave place to a design with which we identify the time, a delicate floral spray tossed on the line of a broken stripe. However endearing this design may be to us, it illustrates the weakening of design under the last king of France.

The sprays of flowers grew smaller and smaller, less and less significant, and were even replaced by little spots. This was surely the decadence of the styles that had made the decoration of France famous throughout the world and for all time. Nevertheless the infinite variety of the motive never erred in taste, and as they suit many a modern room they are freely repeated up to the present day. Another variety of design belonging to the class called pretty to distinguish it from the designs of rich beauty. The French call it *croisillon,* as it is founded on the idea of a background crossed diamond-wise with a line composed of stiff floral forms.

Marie Antoinette and the king lived their lives too much according to their domestic tastes. The private life was more important to them than affairs of the Nation. At times it seemed as though they felt that Versailles was the Nation and nothing mattered that developed outside of its limits. This was illustrated by the interest they took in their little home of the Petit Trianon. They made of it a gem, but the attention centered there might better have been given to the rising tide of rebellion outside the court.

To fit the palace in miniature small furniture was made, small and straight in line. And to suit this small furniture Lyons wove silks of diminutive design. The voluptuous flowers of La Pompadour would have appeared tasteless in contrast to the restraint of the chairs and beds of the new inspiration. And, coming down to the present day we can rejoice in this reduction in size of furniture and silk designs, for we have come into an era of smaller rooms—in towns at least—

and furniture in small scale suits them best. One might say with truth that a greater modesty prevailed in design, and this was due to the lessened extravagance of the court under Louis XVI. No longer a lavish king and a masterful courtesan ruled royal residence and affairs of the State. La Pompadour was deposed and died in 1764. Madame du Barry's influence was nil after the king's death in 1774 although she lived on to endure the wrecking of her home, the villainy of Zamora, the theft of her prodigious casket of jewels, and finally the tumbril and the guillotine.

With the death of Louis XV the artists sought a novelty to place before his successor, and what more natural than that they should develop a style in accord with indications of a dainty taste asserted by Marie Antoinette even while she was but the Dauphiness. So to the naturalistic was added the classic Greek.

The naturalistic meant not only the use of flowers as they grow, represented in the three dimensions. Into this garden of bloom was introduced a whole world of little animals, the familiar little animals associated with man. Oudry seized on these, and Huet, and drew innumerable designs for fabrics, particularly

149

the printed ones, which we shall consider later at greater length.

The mock farm of Marie Antoinette in which she played beside the Trianon was taken as a subject, and to this is attributed the fantastic scenes including cows and goats, carts and farming implements—as well as coquettish maids in bouffant "panniers" and youths in suspiciously graceful attire. For it was the sport of royalty that was depicted, not the life of the grubby peasant.

There is a unity about a change in styles; a new note struck, all departments must attune to it their song. So as fabrics grew more chaste in design, all draperies adopted a tasteful and appropriate diminution. Chairs being smaller and more erect, dropped the general use of the loose seat cushion, and returned to the decorum of the firm upholstery of the chairs of Louis XIV. The principle was a little different for upholsterers had grown more adroit and inventive. Upholstery was no longer a novelty as in the Seventeenth Century.

The backs of chairs were built out from the frame, the upholstery forming an angle. In the preceding style the covering fabric was merely stretched over a slightly bulging back. Draperies disappeared from the walls as panels of painting and tapestry took its place. Even the gathered hanging behind the bed's head was rejected, for the bed itself was built high and uphol-stered. It became fashionable to cover the entire bed-stead with damask, concealing all the wood-work with silk drawn tightly over the wooden frame. Both head and foot-board were thus brought more into promi-nence and took important place, often being of equal height. The beds of languorous ease on which reclined the self-indulgent beauties of the Louis XV epoch had left off altogether the obstacle of a foot-board that the richness of the brocade coverlet might flow uninter-rupted from pillow to floor "like roses heaped on the beloved's bed." But now it was restored, and shared the silken upholstery of the coverlet.

Mahogany beds had often a mere frame for head and foot-boards, and these were filled in with silk panels. Curtains for the bed must by the very nature of things be somewhat alike all through the ages when hung from a square canopy or frame of wood. Tall posts must sustain them at the foot for safety's sake and around the square the curtains must be disposed in sufficient fulness to be half drawn at night. But variety is given by the lambrequin. In the time of Louis XVI this was either a simple fall of ungathered stuff, or was of an inconspicuous festooning. In the former case it was much decorated with galloon. Indeed galloon was indispensable as a decoration on all beds. The coverlet was incomplete without it, for it headed the full flounce of the sides and formed a square or other device in the center. It made the use of taffeta more decorative than even a figured silk. Pillows on beds were deemed too mussy and replaced by the neatness of stiff artificial rolls.

Curtains for windows partook of the simplicity of the curtains for the bed. They were never very heavy, but followed consistently the lightness of the mode prevailing near the end of the Eighteenth Century. If the lambrequin was played with, it was always done in grace and suppleness of effect. The flat band was used when ornamented with galloon and more particularly favored when its lower line was shaped in shallow curves.

The window with arched top called for a treatment

all its own, something that would fall straight at candle-light to shut out the shades of night, the peeping eye of passers-by and the chill of winter evenings. And thus was invented the ingenious placing of cords and rings which were capable of draping a long straight curtain into graceful festooning.

But all was exquisitely restrained and done by true artistic inspiration. Thus in its perfection the style of Louis XVI was the refinement of things decorative, and unlike most styles will bear repeating through the ages. It clashes with nothing; it is ever companionable. If this style was abused during the aberration of the Victorian era it but shared the fate of the preceding styles and suffered less.

It must not be supposed that all textiles of the time were patterned. It was an era of the strong appreciation of plain velvets. The Lyons mills were then turning out a weave adapted to the uses of the day, a lighter weave than that of the Renaissance, when pile was deep and thick. Those were meant for use on heavy furniture without other upholstery than cushions thrown upon the wood, and for hangings to soften the bare stone walls of the fortress-palace. The velvets of the Eighteenth Century had a pile both close and short and thus the fabric had lightness and pliability. All velvets prior to the beginning of the Nineteenth Century were of single width, and show by their selvedge the irregularity of the hand-worked loom.

The use of textile in the periods of decoration named for Louis XV and Louis XVI is noticeably similar with the one exception of tapestries, which declined in size as hangings and became important as furniture coverings. Their heavy masses were even reduced to lightness by simulations. Thus came the tapestry door frame called a *cantonnière,* and the woven imitation of draped and fringed lambrequins for windows and for beds. Art went astray in designing these, yet they dressed many a lovely room in the second half of the Eighteenth Century. They suggest a fabric sprinkled with roses in natural colors, bordered with heavy bullion fringe and hung in a cascade, but the deception could never deceive and the irregular edge was an anomaly. They do, however, show us the preference in those days for shallow drapery with superficially looped scarfs or lambrequins.

The fabrics of Louis XV altered in design from flat

formality of large pattern to sprays and masses of flowers in naturalistic presentation. These rich flowers were too lovely not to be displayed. They were like the Pompadour herself, who flaunted her beauty before the court. And so these flowers of luxuriant growth woven of many-colored silks and glistening with gold, were hung in more open folds than the straight-hung curtains of the earlier day.

The fashion being for curved lines, curtains were ballooned by means of clever looping and thus wider spaces of the fabric were displayed. This obtained for windows and for beds, or wherever a curtain was hung, but on beds the best effects were won, for the Louis XV bed is so beautiful a conception that it is no wonder the state bed-room remained long in fashion as a room where visitors were expected to enter. The fancy of the artist plays about the canopied bed, the canopy which is but a crown, and places there the playful *amorini* whose presence helps to make of the draperies a mass of tinted clouds, the flattering setting of a beauty of the court.

Round-topped windows were draped in two ways, either with a short-looped lambrequin, or with very long curtains with cunningly arranged rings and cords which drew up a drapery in the day and let it fall straight at night.

But call to mind the seats of the Louis XV style, including the Regency, and one realizes that it was the beauty of the silken textiles that kept the cushioning flat and unbroken by any sort of tufting. The chair seat and also that of the popular chaise-longue was often fitted with square cushions, but the foundation on which they were laid was utterly unlike that on which loose cushions were used in the time of the Renaissance. Then it was laid on wooden seats; now it was laid on a silk-covered canvas which was stretched over the frame, a manner which has not yet been changed.

The backs were in all cases stuffed, but not too obviously, the stuffing sloping easily toward the carved wood frame until it reached only the thickness of the silk which was displayed upon it. This silk—or any other covering, petit point, tapestry or leather—was secured by a row of brass-headed tacks placed close together. The seat also avoided all appearance of being over-stuffed or heaped up in the middle. Many an antique chair of modern upholstery has been robbed of all its charm by a simple disregard of the outline of the stuffing in seat and back.

Ladies' dresses were amazing in the amount of material they contained and displayed. As curtains were made to puff themselves balloon-like the dresses of the time were distended by hoops, and all this yard-age of rich silk had to be accommodated when madame sat at cards. The upholstering of the little chairs without arms, and with but small back supports was also simple and restrained. Chairs of the period of Louis XV changed as markedly as all other decorative matter, in this age of unreasoning beauty. Whereas the front arm support had formerly followed the line of the front leg, making a firm and symmetric design, it now slipped half way to the chairback. But this was accomplished with so much of grace and cunning that its loss of balance was lost in the line of beauty.

And what was the reason for the change? The old one of woman's dress. The wide panniers with hoops were thrown into ungovernable pranks if a lady tried to compress them within the arms of a chair. So the arms were set back that madame might be more at her ease and might better display the elegance of her silks.

Even as late as this Eighteenth Century no distinction was made between materials for dress and materials for decoration. The sharp distinction between the two which prevails in our own times was then non-existent. But those fashions for preposterous volume were of a picturesqueness that we of a practical age can never achieve. We can only revel in their beautiful display at a fancy dress ball or in the theater.

Lyons became the silk center of the world. It was she who furnished the silk for the prodigal uses of the Eighteenth Century in France. Strange it seems to us to consider that the tens of thousands of weavers in Lyons worked at home. They took from the factory the thread ready for weaving and returned with the completed textile. That was before the days of Jacquard's loom. Apropos, the selvedge of these handsome silks has always the delightful irregularity given by the touch of the human hand, but never given by the machine.

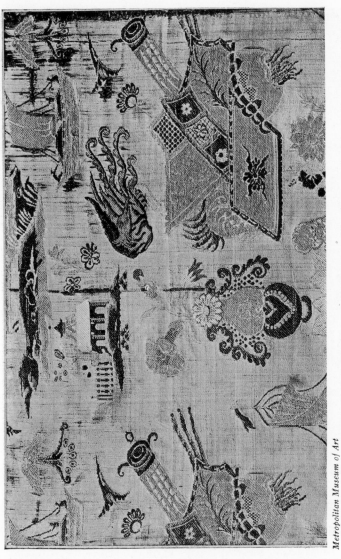

FRENCH, EIGHTEENTH CENTURY CHINESE DISTANTLY COPIED, BLUE, RED, GOLD

LOUIS XIV BROCADE OF FLORAL FORMS COMBINED
WITH LACE

CHAPTER XI

THE DIRECTORY AND THE EMPIRE

IT is bound to come again, a deserved appreciation of the classic styles of the Directory and the Empire. It is amazing that so much beauty could fall into desuetude, could be absolutely neglected by decorator and client.

In its highest expression it showed a refinement that was Greek. But as it depended on an intellectual understanding of such refinement it easily fell into abominable travesty when used by those of little talent, and in its decadence it is truly execrable.

To awaken interest and to inspire admiration consider the artists who executed the style. They were the same talented men who invented the daintiest fancies for the furnishings called after Louis XVI. They merely executed old tricks with new symbols, to suit new political conditions. It was the business of the army of men who had worked in the furniture and textile factory established by Louis XIV in his forceful youth, to please the monarch and his favorites, up to the time when the Revolution obliterated all as being unworthy of the idealists who saw in beauty only corruption. The women of the people who sat knitting by the guillotine, what to them were the bronzes, marquetry, brocades, tapestries conceived by artists in the apartments of the Louvre and executed by the Gobelins factory? They saw in these things but the toys of an aristocracy which drove gorgeous coaches over their children in the narrow village streets. As they hated these haughty tyrants, so they hated all evidences of their luxury and taste.

Factories stopped, bonfires burned up collected bibelots, and artists hid themselves, all atremble lest they be guillotined because a talent existed within their consciousness which could not be plucked out. Those were terrible times for artists, for the artist, after all, was the affair of royalty and aristocracy.

When red rags were waved and death awaited all who could be found guilty of favoring the finer interests of life, what could a designer of panniers—fleuris and ribbon-knots do but burn his brushes and dirty his hands in their cinders to prove himself a glorious com-

mon laborer emancipated from the fripperies of aristocratic taste.

The idol Napoleon rose from the ashes of the burned-
out passion of France. Not even the reddest hater
of the well-born could find any trace of aristocracy
in the family of Bonaparte, which produced many sons
on the island of Ajaccio. Having no ideals of art, it
was inevitable that under the early days of Napoleon's
power the arts remained feeble. Ajaccio has never
been regarded an art center, so we imagine the Bonaparte family as conducting life in a stucco house very
practically with their esthetic needs furnished by the
local producers.

This, instead of making the victorious Napoleon regard beauty in home and palace as unnecessary, made
him keen as the veriest snob to embellish the interiors
where he lived and ruled. That is one of the most
delightful weaknesses of Napoleon, that he showed
himself as human as any lesser man when it came to
giving himself airs. All the softer things and esthetic
that had not embellished the days of his youth he was
eager to own and exhibit as his accustomed habit. The
irreverence of the present day might lead one to whis-

per a word about the traditional airs of the beggar a-horseback. However, once interested in art, the new master of France rapidly developed a taste which could only be gratified by such acts as dethroning the four bronze horses from the Piazza San Marco at Venice and trotting them off to Paris.

And thus came a better day for the artists in decoration. They crept from corners of concealment, sniffed the inspiring air of a revival and soon were put to work at their old ateliers.

But with a canny sense of fitness and flattery they threw away old models and invented new. The spirit of the times had changed and must be reflected. Two reasons. It seemed an unnecessary excitement to the sensitive nerves of the makers of the Revolution to commence duplication of the luxuries of the hated aristocrat. Also, it seemed a wise move to flatter the present Leader of France by forming a style which would be a constant reminder to a victorious people that because of a great commander France was gradually becoming the greatest world-power.

Every military exploit of Napoleon was taken as a decorative inspiration. If there were no imperious

VELVET BROCADE LOUIS XIV, THE LACES OF
THE DAY INSPIRED THE SMALL MOTIVES

VELVET BROCADE LOUIS XIV. COMPARE THIS NATURALISTIC
DRAWING WITH PREVIOUS STYLES

courtesans to inspire as in kings' times, there were designs in plenty to take from conquered countries, and these served the artists for some of the most delightful small motives ever inspired. On fabrics for decoration there was, for instance, the bee loved by the Emperor. It might be thought a bit of childishness for him to choose the humming insect of a garden, a turning back of his thoughts to childhood in Ajaccio—for what child does not love to watch a bee suck honey and menace a sting the while? But to Napoleon the bee meant the forcing of Rome to her knees before him. The powerful Roman family of the Barberini, aristocrats, patrons of art—it was from them he snatched their inherited emblem, making it his own with the victor's arrogance.

The artists took it with avidity, had it embroidered in gold all over costly velvets and brocades with an N of great conspicuousness in close association. Thus was advertised the capitulation of a family so great that Rome itself was included in the fall.

The campaign extended to Egypt. There was rare material for the designer, something exotic, piquant. The exquisite trifles of the last two styles of France

163

had reached their highest expression in the work of Lancret, Huet and their followers. Egypt was a whole book of exotic motifs as yet untouched. Artists who please king or emperor must have ever a trick of flattery. It was probable that Napoleon would think it pleasant to wake in the morn to the sight of a pair of bronze sphinxes on his bed-head or one of lotus columns supporting his mirror. But the Egyptian inspiration never got very far, it was confined to small decorative motifs. Great use was made of these in gilt-bronze ornaments on furniture, taking the place of the carving so freely used in previous styles.

But it was exactly these little gold-bronze ornaments which suggested the small figures brocaded in silks for hangings and coverings. With a history of Napoleon in hand one can almost date the furniture and hangings of the short fifteen years of his dominance by the display of symbols pertinent to his exploits.

Just why conquerors take to themselves the emblems of the conquered is a matter of psychology. It would seem that Napoleon should have forced the lily of France upon Italy, Spain, Egypt, Austria, rather than to adopt for his own the emblems of those countries.

But that, as said before, is one of the ways of all conquerors through history.

But in spite of new blood in the way of fresh conquests, the great dominant throughout the Napoleonic period was Greek. Not so much in the history of wars is the reason found for this as in the story of the excavations in Pompeii and Herculaneum, and those Greek ruins were in Italy the subjugated. The inspiring places were a source of joy to all of France who cared for the arts—and who in France is born without artistic appreciation!

It was in these years, the late Eighteenth and early Nineteenth Centuries that Pompeii was relieved of the weight of ashes under which Vesuvius had buried her, and there lay revealed a city built by Greeks of the colony in Italy. And Greek Pompeii furnished the fundamentals of the styles which we name after the French political periods of the Directory and the Empire.

Discoveries in the pretty town were begun long before, had their influence in England under the Adam Brothers, in France under Louis XVI; but in Napoleon's time a more intense consistency in style was the

rule. Also a certain austerity crept in. The furniture
and draperies of the time became so rigid as to seem
to scorn mere personal luxury.

It was in the decorative detail that the period ex-
celled. The luxurious sweep of a chaise-longue or
the cajoling undulations of a bed à la Pompadour vanished utterly. The square lines of the Empire chair
were built for a severer state of mind, a more evident
rectitude of the spirit.

The bed became square as a box, and in spite of its
decorations suggested severity. The silks which dressed
it took on the same simplicity. The brocade cover of
the bed was in itself a sign of the wish to destroy all
evidence of an abolished hereditary royalty. Tightly
stretched across the mattress it is tucked in behind the
side boards of the bed, and at top and bottom as well,
with a look of absolute permanency. To complete the
rigid perfection, a roll is laid at either end, cylinders
one might call them, and there you have a bed of
dignity and symmetry, but not one that in any way
suggests repose until the housemaid has torn away
cover and rolls and displayed softness beneath.

But what style lurks in all this stiffness, and how

beautiful are all details! The silks present a field of satin on which a diminutive and isolated small figure is thrown in regularity of spacing. The figure is the star or the Barberini bee, or the honeysuckle or palmette of the Greek convention. More elaborate brocades were made in Lyons which carried some of the traditions of the Louis XVI style inasmuch as these were founded on the Greek. Borders for velvet or silk brocades were woven for use as edging to these when made into hangings or when fixed flat upon the wall. These borders magnified and diversified the palmette and the honeysuckle, but sadly altered them. Or the textiles were woven in stripes of satin and plain silk. These stripes are of equal width and of the same color. Gone are the masses of flowers brocaded in countless tones, or the broken stripes of many colors which were flounced and gallooned to make lovely the bed of a few years earlier.

Beds to be in fashion were placed against the wall, which made the silk-covered rolls almost a necessity for symmetry's sake. Yet, as a bed needs to make a distinct effect against the wall the fashion was to hang a drapery behind it. Even a baldaquin was used as a point from which the drapery was hung, but infinitely simple were all lines.

Against the wall the flat drapery was allowed three box-plaits, one in the center, one at each end, with the merest suggestion of "eased" material between. Plain satin or dull silk served, unless the bed-cover demanded a repetition of its own pattern.

Walls made background for ladies witty and ladies pretty, so were allowed the effects which never fail to flatter women's appearance—the draping of silk. But this draping had none of the graceful abandon of former days. It was copied in effect from Pompeian frescoes, from the paintings so recently exposed by the director of the Italian workman's shovel.

And the result was an entrancing classicism. To begin with, the silk for hanging was plain, relying on its own lustrous quality and on its color for shading. It was hung from the top of the cornice, which in itself was a mere molding, in the simplest manner possible, that is, in far-spaced single box-plaits. The manner of attaching to the wall was entirely concealed. The scantiness of the stuff kept it in the desired straight lines, yet folds enough were apparent to make the room soft and colorful without a suggestion of the luxury which leads to decadence. Against such a background were grouped the ladies of Josephine's court, amid those simple silks were perpetrated the badinage, and the cutting wit for which it was celebrated, and here the painters, David, Ingres and a host of others caught inspiration for their lovely portraits.

The men who had been designing delightful trifles such as a tangle of garden tools and flowers, of musical instruments and ribbons, for silk weavers and workers in ormolu or gilt bronze, began forthwith to compose on lines of the Greek. Thus it is that one finds on the furniture metal ornaments of a perfection unexcelled. The little motifs are hand chiseled after models drawn by the best of artists, executed by talented workers, and are almost worthy to be classed among jewelry. In their best development the Directory and Empire styles cause thrills of delight to the appreciative and discriminating. They have dignity and symmetry in the larger lines, and in detail are unsurpassed for delicacy of workmanship.

This condition required a change in stuffs. If the

object was to center the eye on the beauty of the *orfèvrerie,* the jewel-like incrustations of gilt on mahogany, then simplicity of woven design followed naturally. The colors of these silks were as thoroughly different from those of the Eighteenth Century as was the drawing. The graded tones all disappeared and colors were frankly red or blue, green, yellow or brown. The red was deep, the blue was sapphire, the green was clear, neither tinged with yellow nor sharpened with blue; the yellow also clear. In fact subtlety in color had disappeared.

Behold France, then, trying to eschew beauty as more or less a sin against the new order, yet at the same time eager to express her people's innate spirit, her god-given talent for enrapturing the eye. The early days of the Empire saw the necessity of a strictness in outward appearance, a stiff rectitude a lucidity without shading. Napoleon having come from a simple life was in the proper form to continue it. He had larger matters in hand than the mere making home beautiful even though that home were the palace of a dethroned king.

Affairs of beautifying were in the hands of the

FRENCH BROCADE OF THE EIGHTEENTH CENTURY
WITH THE HEAVY-HEADED FLOWERS DEVELOPED
UNDER THE PERIOD NAMED FOR LOUIS XV

FRENCH BROCADE, TIME OF LOUIS XV, MULTICOLORED
AND SHOWING THE OVERDEVELOPMENT OF FLORAL
NATURALISM

artists. I imagine these men as having been in hiding
in garrets or in farms, and of peeping timidly out when
the storm was over, and of trembling lest their hands
betray the old methods of design once so acceptable to
Court and aristocracy. The spirit of the times must
be followed. Formal and cold the Pompeian model
seemed perhaps but how safe it was. Even the arro-
gant citizen, the class-leveler of a few years back, could
not find in it reminders of the hated Eighteenth Century masters.

Napoleon as Emperor adhered ever to the new style,
which then passed from cold thin austerity into a more
elegant phase, but ever were present the Greek outlines and Greek details of restraint and beauty. On
his brow he wore not the crown of kings but the
laurel wreath of the Greek victor, when standing for his
portrait as monarch.

When wealth and luxury and a proper court of wits
and beauties had been established around the Emperor, a greater elegance was demanded. It was then
that Madame Récamier flashed her wit and beauty in
the crowd, the beautiful Pauline Bonaparte undulated
through gay soirées, Madame de Staël showed her

bright mind by tongue and pen, and the Empress herself headed the circle.

Rooms where these famous folk foregathered were cold and formal when decorated only with bands of frescoed Greek ornament. Something softer and more intimate was required, some treatment that warmed the salon but still kept the flavor of the Greek. But the silks hung over the walls still keep the idea of restraint and severity. Windows that broke into the walls were hung with short valances like the wall drapery, but on either side fell a fringed cascade like a jabot of flatness and restraint.

Who could avoid noticing the similarity between such drapings and the scant dresses of the time? The Greek ideal furnished the inspiration for both. The celebrated portrait of Madame Récamier by David might have been taken from a Pompeian fresco. Madame de Staël was wearing such a costume and shining in such a room when she evoked from Napoleon his surprising reply. "Whom, Sire, do you consider the most important woman in France?" "She who bears the greatest number of children, Madame," he replied to the childless intellectual.

Going back to the subject of coverings for chairs, most important of all were the tapestries. The Napoleonic era is generally considered negligible as to the manufacture of tapestries. That is true as to the scenes made for hangings. A few of these were woven, precise and exact in design and execution, but mainly lacking in charm. Moreover they had no borders. But the furniture covers of the time are marvels in design and in technique of weaving. The favored factory was Beauvais. The artists who produced the most exquisite design of the Louis XVI expression turned their facile talent to the creation under the new manner. In place of flowers and fripperies, they drew Greek amphoræ and vases, instead of small animals they drew Greek medallions, surrounding all with a formal border in which the palmette played its part.

And the hand of the weaver had not lost its cunning. Indeed it seemed rather to have it in greater development. Never have finer nor more charming tapestry coverings been woven than those of the Empire period. They show the greatest achievements in design and execution. Fortunate are those who possess them as they display their thrilling beauty against the lightly carved and decorated mahogany of the frames. As for colors, the uncompromising primal colors shown in silk are absent here, and instead we have a blending of as lovely tones as ever pleased a king's favorite in the preceding century.

FRENCH BROCADE OF EIGHTEENTH CENTURY, STYLE OF
LOUIS XV

GALLOON AND TASSELS FOR UPHOLSTERY OF THE
EIGHTEENTH CENTURY

CHAPTER XII

THE story of tapestries follows the story of art, for artists have ever furnished the designs for the weavers. It has many another story woven into its texture and these all have to do with men and women whose lives even in retrospect are vivid and important.

The art of tapestry reached three great developments. The first we call Gothic, the second Renaissance, the third Gobelins or Eighteenth Century. This neat condensation of terms requires amplifying, for the words themselves are misleading. Gothic has nothing to do with the Goths—a savage people who harried Europe in the early Middle Ages. And Gobelins is used indiscriminately for all tapestries of the Seventeenth and Eighteenth Centuries, wherever woven, by those who are more careless than specific.

To make the story hold together and to make it rich with human interest, we follow the art with profitable respect to chronology. As ever when the inception of an art is sought, the mind and imagination have to fly

175

nimbly back over the centuries to pick up half-forgotten facts and romance.

Beginning with the weave itself, we are balked in our investigations backwards by finding it to be prehistoric. More interesting it is to take up the subject at a date where documents are plenty, that is in the countries and centuries when mankind in Europe developed luxury and decoration beyond the needs of primitive people.

The weave is primarily the simple one of a warp crossed by a weft thrown under and over, with unvarying regularity, the weft threads being pushed down into place with a sort of comb to cover completely the warp. The great difference between this fabric and a plain cloth is that the shuttles are many, each carrying a different color and rarely fly all across the loom, but each is stopped at will and its direction reversed when desired. This simple expedient, with the multiplication of the shuttles or bobbins which carry the weft, makes the fabric we call tapestry.

Even the word tapestry is capable of many definitions, but we use it to denote the hand-woven pictured cloths. Indeed to those who love old tapestries there is revolt in the heart when some shopman shows wall-paper or goods by the yard under the name of tapestry. The French have a way of calling all tapestries Gobe-lins, even those made hundreds of years before the Gobelins Factory was founded. And that too might confuse a novice in studying or buying.

The weave is the same as that employed by the Egyptians and Copts, Second to Seventh Centuries, and of which we have such fascinating remains in our great collections. Almost all of those remains are concerned with garments, and are but trimmings so to speak, but of late much larger fragments have been found which appear to be parts of hangings or couch covers, and these in design are startlingly like sections of foliage from the great Flemish tapestries of the early Fourteen Hundreds. They are not flat leaf patterns, but have the three-dimensional quality to such a degree that they seem ready to flutter at the lightest stirring of a breeze. In color they are like the richest tints of autumn. One wonders how a weaver in warm North Egypt could picture the glowing October foliage of Canadian forests.

Another wonder are the tapestries from ancient Peru, many of which were woven contemporaneously with the Coptic. Some were woven before the conquest of the aborigines by the Incas, and some after, but the weave is ever the same. Indeed, pictured cloths could not have been made with any other weave, for the intricacies of method allow the greatest liberty of portrayal.

Slight evidences of tapestry weave are shown wherever ancient fabrics have been preserved, but as time has destroyed all except those which have lain buried in dry desert countries, we have an insufficient amount to create interest except in the breast of the archeologist. Therefore let us pick up the art in Europe in the century before the Renaissance, and for convenience' sake we will call it Gothic.

It takes us to the North, to Belgium then called Flanders. It seems as though this country had for years been preparing for the art and for the ability to produce the prodigious quantity of tapestries she was called upon to supply to the world as soon as her great art became known. Flanders was the wool-producing country of the world. England under Elizabeth was her rival, but prior to that Flanders was pre-eminent. Her weavers were the most able, their goods the best. Partly this was because of the system of guilds that not only united weavers in a common interest but that gave them the highest ideals in quality of work.

The guild was made of master-workmen who owned their own shop, made and sold their own goods. Under them were the apprentices who must work many years and become superlatively proficient before they might themselves become master-workmen. These apprentice lads and men, however gay a group they may look in pictures and on the operatic stage, must have felt that servitude was long when independence was not obtained under fifteen years of service. They were kept back thus long to prevent too many shops with a consequent glut of goods on the market.

It was the business of the cloth makers' guild in Flanders to see that high standards were maintained, that dyes were unfadable and pleasing to the eye, that yarn was evenly spun, even that the proper sort of sheep were grazing on the low-lands, the sheep that provided the wool.

There was never a big town that did not have as its two most important buildings the cathedral and the cloth-house. And almost as much labor and taste

179

was expended on one as on the other. Cloth-making and religion seem to have been the two great interests of the people.

Tapestries came because they were needed. They were not merely a new manner for the expression of artists. They were needed primarily to make home a comfortable retreat. In those days houses were not warm nests of paneled walls and central heating. They were stone inside as well as out, and heated no more than an open fire can heat, with not too many fires at that. The winter wind whistled insinuatingly over the shoulders of those who sat beside the wall, and whined through the cracks of doors as it blew fresh from snowy reaches onto man as he reclined in hours of ease.

Some warm and cozy protector was needed, so the big hanging tapestry was invented. Probably cloth was tried at first, but even if it mitigated the icy blast its dark dye dressed the rooms with gloom and with monotony. Something of gay color, of pictorial inter- est, was desired, demanded. And so the ancient weave was called to help, artists drew pictures or cartoons to copy, looms of huge size were constructed, and with enormous courage the weavers inaugurated an art whose future importance they could not possibly imagine.

Flanders throughout the tapestry weaving centuries had a marvelously varied history. At the inception of this new industry she was at peace. Her earlier history was concerned with Charlemagne whose name appears in the annals of all states. When his great Empire was dismembered in 843, Flanders was set apart to form a buffer state that should keep France and Germany apart. But the rulers who most affected the art of tapestry weaving were the Dukes of Burgundy and Louis XI.

Appreciation of the hangings was immediate, and the first to receive them were the rulers in command. Tapestries came into a cold gray world and immediately there was warmth and beauty. Flowers bloomed, trees bore bright fruit on leafy branches, playful animals leaped about, and exquisite ladies hesitated in the greenwood as though in ecstasy at its loveliness. There are still left a few of these early tapestries, notably one of that fascinating Isabeau of Bavaria whose naughty history as a queen is so far away that one can relish it with propriety. It will be remembered that she was exceeding fair, that she wrecked every man who looked into her eyes, that she went to Paris for her marriage to Charles VI thus becoming Queen of France, and that she died in 1435. No wonder the artists made a tapestry cartoon of her, as she with three or four companions strayed through an enchanted wood rich with the foliage and the flowers of spring, neither of the men who walked with her in the wood being her husband the king. The elegant slenderness of the figures, the grace of the composition and its power to convert the beholder into a member of that sylvan party, make of it one of the loveliest of Gothic tapestries. Mr. Edson Bradley once lent it to the Metropolitan Museum for a year, thus giving transport of delight to the appreciative and causing anguish in the hearts of the envious. It belongs to the class of secular subjects, which were always treated with a loving touch, as though artist and weaver were within the realm of personal experiences on which it were happiness to dwell.

Subjects of the early tapestries sometimes reflect the thought of the day and include representations of events contemporary. Of these there are far too few, for wars, and classic and religious history were considered a more scholarly and dignified field. Religious subjects were paramount. This was but natural at a time when theatrical representations were limited to morality plays. Far from merry it must have been to repair to the playhouse of a winter's night to witness in a dim light the struggle of man against the dragon Vice, and the punishments of that same man when he lost the battle. Religion being his only help, the moral was drawn with heavy emphasis.

And thus it came that religious or morality subjects were oftenest on the loom in the Fourteenth and Fifteenth Centuries. Another reason for this is found in the art of painting. For long the monasteries had been the museums, the strongholds in which were deposited the treasures even of kings, when war was rampant. And for long the painter monks had been the most productive of the artists. That their work was in miniature lessens not its beauty of composition and of color.

Flanders contributed then her most famous artists, the Van Eycks and Hans Memling. Their work was but an enlargement of the monk's missal. It preserved the spirit of the miniature although its scale was larger. And on their designs the early Flemish weavers depended for their best inspiration in religious subjects.

Just for the sake of being informed one must know of the fancy for depicting the Apocalypse and of the marvelous production under that head which hangs in the cathedral of Angers and to see which many a tourist—I had almost said pilgrim—takes a long journey. It was woven by Nicholas Bataille—in France—and is one of the great textiles of the world. Thus we touch on a place of weaving outside of Flanders, France of the Northern districts.

The Life of Christ, the Life of the Virgin, became enormously popular subjects as the weavers increased in numbers and in ability. The artist who drew the cartoon then invented a charming and ingenious method of including many scenes on one tapestry. There were made many sets of many pieces by order of great patrons, but often came a request for a single piece to hang in home or chapel, and on this both artist and weaver lavished the best of his talent.

The space of the cloth was divided into as many fields as were required, by means of architectural helps; slender columns supporting arches, thrust their upright line between the scene of the Virgin's birth and the Visitation, between the Coronation and the Assumption, and all with beautiful regard to symmetry and scale. The various scenes were executed by the most talented of the weavers, those who were true artists, and much gold was introduced. For us who are concerned with all textiles, not tapestries alone, it is interesting to note the patterns of the robes in which all the important personages were dressed. Velvets and brocades are indicated just as they were coming into Venice from the Ottoman Empire, just as the looms of Genoa were newly weaving them.

These many-scened tapestries of the late Fifteenth Century reached perfection. Nothing has ever been executed in tapestry weaving so exquisite, so high in art. Not only have they the beauty of a painting, but they have an inherent power to hold the silent attention of their beholders until the spirit of religion that called them into existence seizes upon the spirit, and one falls into a mood of worship. The highest example of this variety of tapestry is one called after a former possessor, the great art connoisseur Cardinal Mazarin, he who helped to form the character of the young Louis XIV. It is said to have been woven in Arras for Ferdinand and Isabella of Spain. Mr. Pierpont Morgan brought it to America and it now sheds its undying glory on the collection of Mr. Joseph Widener of Philadelphia. For several years by Mr. Morgan's generosity it hung in the Metropolitan Museum guarded by a Hollander who loved it as a child. Irrelevant it may be to mention such a circumstance, but is it not a proof of the undying power of the old tapestry weavers and their works to speak to man throughout the ages and even to men of our own time? The life of Moses, the lives of saints were all depicted at this time of perfect weaving, of perfect cooperation between artist, master-weaver, assistants and dyers.

Gold thread was lavishly used to heighten effects. It is interesting to note that in these threads there is a connection between East and West. The manner of manufacture was to lay gold leaf on a thin animal membrane where it readily adhered, and to cut this in infinitely fine strips which were then wound on silk or linen threads for weaving. Gold of Cyprus was the name of this importation. It was of such value that when a hanging was ordered a separate contract or stipulation was made for the gold, according to the amount introduced into the weaving.

The French call millefleurs the charming tapestries of leaves and flowers and little animals that set a-tingling the emotions of any one who had a childhood in the big out of doors which is the kingdom of childhood. Under the Burgundian Dukes many of these were woven, and the pretty habit continued until the next century—the Sixteenth. To distinguish the earliest regard the size of the leaves and fruit. They are nearly on the scale of nature, and resemble their prototype of certain generous Coptic weaving. Then they appear but scantily, peeping from behind a scene in the thorny aspect of a holly-bush or the mounting stem of a rose-tree, while overhead are the thrusting branches of trees rich with fruit. Among this naturalistic high-colored vegetation are personages of romance, and perhaps a peep of their distant towers.

Far smaller in scale and daintier are the millefleurs tapestries of the later years of the century. Sometimes these tapestries are solid fields of verdure without the interruption of human figures. It is as though a master weaver had taken a day off from his work at the loom and had thrown himself on the blossoming earth of early June, there to revel in the sights of the country round about Arras. All through the tapestry the hares are peeping and little dogs are smelling them out, while a fox or two runs wisely to cover among the leafage. It is not a scene, no personages distract the attention, it is simply a few square yards of nature. Such tapestries are not unlike the rugs of Persia woven at about that time.

In the Cluny Museum at Paris are the very loveliest possible tapestries of this variety. If one wishes to be transported backward through history and arrive at the enchantment of ancient times an hour may well be spent with them. I refer to the set called The Lady and the Unicorn—La Dame et la Licorne.

Usually the foundation color of the millefleurs tapestry of this order is of a deep green, almost black, which scarcely shows between the flowers of the field and wood, but this set at the Cluny has the rare distinction of being woven with a background of red, that tempered red of the old weavers, mellow but not self-assertive. This alone would mark it as a rarity, but it is in the composition of the scenes we see the skill of both cartoonist and weaver. A lady of high degree and her attendant maid of honor are the personages and accompanying them are two heraldic animals, a lion and a unicorn upholding banners. There are accessories in each scene—in one a harp, in another a falcon, indicating music and the sport of the aristocrat. But it is the power to excite the imagination that is the chief charm of the tapestries of this superlative set.

They illustrate another matter also, that the looms of Arras were not alone in their production of ideal tapestries, for these were woven in France. Through their perfection of weave and beauty of design they suggest that France was more able than Arras at least in this particular type of tapestry. But a few years later the looms of Flanders produced hangings of another style which have never been surpassed in workmanship or designs.

While considering the subjects for the cartoons—the cartoon being the artist's drawing which it was the weaver's work to translate into wool and silk and

metal—one sees in the battle scenes a sign of the times.
Peace was ever of short duration in Flanders. There
was war with England, there were the struggles of the
Dukes of Burgundy for domination, and their rule
from about 1400 to 1477, and after that the seizure of
Arras by the tyrant Louis XI. Besides the conflicts
consequent upon this there were the Crusades in which
Flanders took part.

The Dukes of Burgundy almost rivaled the Kings of
France in power and in the size of the territory over
which they reigned. The nobles of France were rightly
feared by the king, they were not mere courtiers led
by him. The Duke of Burgundy called Philip the
Hardy was the first to govern Flanders. He being the
son of that King of France called John the Good had
perhaps the right of royalty to step in. It was he who
arranged peace with the English who were then in
power in Flanders, and it was he who patronized with
enthusiasm the industrial art of tapestry weaving.
This was about 1400 A.D. The Flemish were already
heavy producers. It is recorded that this same Philip
the Hardy made gifts of tapestries to the English who
thus increased a knowledge of the art in England.

FRENCH BROCADE OF THE EIGHTEENTH CENTURY WHEN WAVY PARALLELS WERE
FORMED OF TWISTED LINES OF ORNAMENT. THIS STYLE IS CALLED AFTER LOUIS
XV AND LOUIS XVI

FRENCH SILKS OF LATE EIGHTEENTH CENTURY. LOUIS
XVI OR MARIE ANTOINETTE

Philip was made Lord of the Comité of Artois which included the town of Arras.

John-without-Fear was the next of these vigorous swash-buckling Dukes of the Middle Ages, and it was his pleasure to command five battle scenes, some such large and complicated scene as that of the Sack of Jerusalem which hangs in the Metropolitan Museum.

Philip the Good governed next. It was he who lent of his tapestries to make gorgeous the streets and bridges of Paris for a royal progress through the city of the young King Louis XI. It was not so very many years later that this insanely cruel king laid plans to weaken Flanders and secure a part of it for himself. All these Burgundians in spite of the size of their possessions (which were almost as large as France, reaching to the east of that country from the Mediterranean to the English Channel) devoted themselves to the now famous industry peculiar to the Comité of Artois. They not only encouraged tapestry commerce with other nations, but laid up for themselves the most amazing lot of woven treasure. This same Philip the Good—they favored descriptive names in those days—owned so many hangings that he had built a storehouse for the safe-keeping of his collection. This was in 1429.

With Charles the Bold the end of the Burgundian rule over the Flemish weavers terminates. Like all the others of his line he gave his patronage to the great artistic industry, and also kept himself supplied. So great was his attachment to his tapestries that he took some about with him wherever he traveled to make more elegant his surroundings.

Louis XI was King. Looking with envy on the rich industrious population of Flanders he determined to conquer it for the aggrandizement of France. He managed by cunning attacks to weaken the country's resistance. When Charles the Bold was lured into battle with the Swiss, Louis XI found his opportunity. The Burgundian was routed and died miserably on the field. Louis XI then attached to himself Artois with its weaving town of Arras. Those who travel today in Berne and in Nancy can get the flavor of those old bellicose times in the Arras tapestries preserved in those towns, the very tapestries taken by Charles the Bold (le Téméraire) to ornament his tent on the field of battle.

Then came evil days for the Flemish weavers, or at least for those of Arras. Louis XI took Arras in 1477, just at the time of her greatest productiveness and skill. His mania was conquest and cruelty, not the arts. The weavers of Arras fled for their lives. Some went across the water to England, many went to France in the northern counties. As a tapestry center Arras was no more, for Artois then belonged to an eccentric French King.

It was at this time that Brussels in Brabant arose as a producer. From that time on until the decadence of about 1550 she was the world's leader. But this is not to forget the tapestry-weaving of northern France. No great center arose there, but many tapestries were nevertheless produced, and these are distinguished by a delightful softness of the fabric, a tender yet honest scale of color, and a display of great individual talent in the design. It is only of late years that these have been separated from Flemish work, therefore many old attributions were mistaken. But now that our eyes are opened we are eager to make amends.

In the middle of the Fifteenth Century all the countries of Europe were interested in the tapestry productions of Flanders and each one established warehouses in Bruges and Ghent.

CHAPTER XIII

THE charm of the very old tapestries depends on their sincerity and simplicity. They have the winsome qualities of naïveté. The cartoons partake of the religious atmosphere of the monastic drawings. Their colors are limited to less than twenty, and the *brèches,* or bobbins, carry only wool. Silk was not yet plentiful enough in Europe to be used in tapestry-weaving, and gold was a rarity—at least it is seldom found in the tapestries left to us.

But quite a different note was struck at the end of the Fifteenth Century. It is as though the makers of tapestry had suddenly stepped from the nursery of their art into the world of wealth and sophistication.

Artists of the first rank drew the cartoon—one might say composed the picture, for what is a cartoon but a painting drawn with an emphasis on technique. The artists are those we know today by the works in our collectors' galleries, Van Eyck, David, Roger Van der

194

Weyden, Bernard Van Orley. Flanders was finishing her period of Gothic painting with a brilliant development that was completely her own, and not imported.

When all the world was showing appreciation of Flemish tapestries, it was not surprising that artists of first rank should contribute their talent. But without the super-weaver the artist's designs were vain. In fact the weaver must himself be an artist. The translation of figures and particularly faces into woven fabric required more than mere manual skill, it involved the sensitive perception of one who was at heart an artist, although he painted no canvases.

The master-weaver, or tapissier, as he was called, executed such tapestries as the Mazarin hanging, where a more careless hand could have ruined the inspired faces of the central group. As such work consumed years of time, the master-weaver cleverly left unimportant areas to his pupils or apprentices. If the center of the field was occupied by an important group of personages, perhaps flanked by two others, these were always the work of the master; but a little scene which filled a corner, or the frame of columns which separated the scenes, were given to the lesser men to weave.

Borders too were their especial province. In the earliest Gothic tapestries the border as such was unknown. In its place was a band of lettering at the top, or the suggestion of a wall at the sides, or of pavement or flower-bed at the base. But late in the Fifteenth Century the border was an accustomed finish to the best hangings. With fine instinct it kept to simple floral motives, and to a subservient width.

Subjects at this time of perfect weaving were very largely religious. Scenes from the life of saints were woven with what seems like religious devotion. Scenes from the life of the day were not the mode, but one can infer much from the details of the religious scenes. It often happened that a dress was true of the time although it draped the figure of an historic personage. These little anachronisms are an amusement in our eyes, not a fault.

Artists could not forever draw pictures of Christ's life, for the fashion of the day was to dwell on the least happy of His hours and days. So to find new subjects yet keep within the religious tradition they turned to the Old Testament and picked up there some tales containing secular interest. Sheba's queen surrounded by

196

elegant wealth of drapery appears before Solomon in all his glory. Esther and Ahasuerus introduce us into royal elegance—Judith and Holofernes also. These biblical characters and their surrounding groups gave chance for displaying the elegance of court life. Incidentally all these men and women of sacred history were attired in the velvet brocades of the late Fifteenth Century. But that as we know detracts nothing from their beauty and adds a bit to humor. Much gold was woven into these matchless tapestries but with charming restraint. It glistens, it never glares; it lights a maiden's tresses or makes brilliant a queen's jewels or coronation robe, but it never reached the obvious display attained in cloth of gold.

Morality subjects extended through this period and reveled in such subjects as a portrayal of The Seven Deadly Sins, the Triumph of Virtue, and other warnings to feeble and tempted mankind. The classic myths of Greece and Rome also had a vogue.

There came a fashion in tapestries less beautiful than these we have been considering, but because so many of them have survived and because Gothic tapestries of almost any sort are so hard to find nowadays, they should be noted. They are mainly composed of figures uniform in size, arranged on the field with due regard to spacing, but almost without accent, so much alike are the personages in size and dress and attitude.

A favorite subject among them is the Court of Love, yet it might as well have been called a Garden Party, or a Reception at the House of a Noble. Young women all dressed alike in heavy draperies and heads coifed after the local fashion of 1500 A.D. stand solidly while young men respectfully address them. As is noticeable in receptions of today the women outnumber the men, and to dispose of these extras they are set in the far background as wall-flowers have ever been.

These tapestries have lost the architectural division of scenes. The exquisite subterfuge of slender Gothic dividing columns has disappeared. The tender treatment of the face which could reproduce the subtlety of human expression is not found here. And one of these tapestries is very like another. Evidently they were made to hang in folds, not stretched like a picture, and when so hung their charm reveals itself. The tall ladies of long straight hanging robes seem actually to sway with animation when the tapestry is moved by a current of air or a restless hand.

Louis XI who denuded Arras of its weavers in 1477, died only six years later, but his acts lived after him. The thousands of workers engaged in the weaving of tapestries many of whom took refuge in Brussels, never returned to their homes. It was due entirely to this emigration that Brussels became the center of the industry and remained for generations the chief city of production. There were other cities at work, but the greatest fame was for Brussels with its Arras weavers.

At this time the weavers in various small towns of northern France were imitating Flanders. Their tapestries form one of the enigmas of the dealer or collector who wishes to place their origin, to attribute them definitely to Lille to Tournai or to some smaller place. Often one can but say with charming inexactness they are French, and let it go at that. But as tapestries have an atmosphere given by the race or the individuals who weave them, these French tapestries have a quality all their own. Were I to try to define it such words would come to mind as suavity, softness, contrasts, harmony, proportion, which all together would mean an originality that emanates from an intelligent instinct for style.

Brussels remained ever true to certain conventions in design, while the French method was freer. Brussels followed long the mode set by the early painters who themselves were bound by convention, and therefore her best masters preserved high excellence. I mention Matsys, Van Eyck and all that band of early artists who produced for their patrons the triptych, or triple, picture for religious uses. It was arranged in three panels, hung together with hinges, and served in a church or at private worship. The master tapissier perhaps had one in his own house and knelt before its scenes of the Life of Christ. It is easy to see how logical it would be for him to put into his weaving the Gothic frame to divide the scenes as in the triptych.

And then came the introduction of a new style of art into the land of the Flemish weavers, the art of Italy's High Renaissance. The perfection of Gothic art had been reached, was in its most lovely flowering at about 1500. Yet in 1518 it was to be pushed into the background and to disappear altogether by reason of

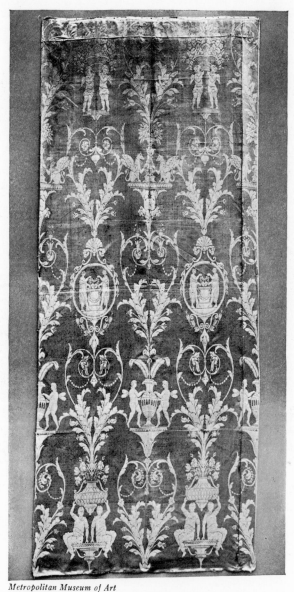

LYONS SILK IN LATE EIGHTEENTH CENTURY
DESIGN WHICH SHOWS THE RETURN TO THE
CLASSIC BEFORE IT STIFFENED INTO THE
EMPIRE

LATE GOTHIC TAPESTRY, ABOUT 1500, WHEN THE GOTHIC
WAS IN FULL FLOWER UNTOUCHED BY THE RENAISSANCE

the cartoons drawn by Raphael which were sent to Brussels for their weaving.

To know what perfection in tapestries means, one should associate freely with such tapestries as that one reproduced here which represents scenes in the Life of the Virgin. The artist who drew the cartoon knew how to express therein a religious fervor and tender sentiment. Apart from that he knew how to keep to the Gothic convention of making many scenes obviously separated, yet of retaining the unity of the whole. Looked at as a single composition its arrangement is without error. And each scene is a completed picture.

The quaint roughness of the earlier Burgundian methods had been outgrown. Even the more finished ones of many personages all on one plane like the Court of Love had been discarded. In place of these, as weavers grew more able, came the light fine texture which alone could portray the designs of the most talented of artists.

Thus came such perfection of Gothic art as that displayed in the old mellow tapestries similar to that pictured here. Each scene is full of an undying beauty that never loses value, whatever style of art may be in vogue. It is tender, appealing, human, besides which it speaks of a more cultivated state of mind than do the earlier works, and includes more indications of elegant living. And over the whole is thrown that atmosphere of devout worship and religious spirit that once expressed itself in the building of the great cathedrals.

Yet in all this improvement in their art—its modernizing, if you like—there appeared no classic or Hellenic details. The far country below the feet of the ascending Virgin is dressed with medieval towers, not Roman remains, the chalice offered the Child in the Adoration is truly Gothic, such as was in use in Flanders in 1500. The separating columns have no trace of Greek invention, but are purely Gothic. And all the rich apparel of the subjects is rich with the designs at that day on the looms of Florence, Venice and the Ottoman Empire, districts which were silk centers of the times.

It is the production of the perfect Gothic tapestry that Italy interrupted when she sent to Brussels the celebrated Raphael cartoons of The Acts of the Apostles. It happened in this wise: a Medici Pope, Leo X, was in the Vatican from 1513 to 1521. Like others of his great family he was a collector and a patron of art. He with all the world knew the perfection of the tapestry-weavers of Brussels, and on finding none in Italy equal to the task of translating into wool and silk the designs of the great master, he despatched the cartoons by special messengers to Flanders.

One can fancy the wonder and consternation of the master weavers on unrolling the great surfaces of life-size figures drawn with free hand after the strong Italian manner. All their work had been on a scale that seemed miniature compared to this, full of almost meticulous detail. Now it would be necessary to loosen the hand, to let lines flow and make the rhythm of moving human bodies apparent.

The work was done. There was no doubt about the ability of the Brussels weavers to follow any type of cartoon. Two years or so the weavers were busy on this set of The Acts of the Apostles which still hangs in the Vatican. And during that time of absorption in the new manner, the old was set aside. And thus came the class of tapestries named for the Renaissance.

Perhaps among the master-weavers were some who wept for the destruction of the Gothic. Perhaps there are some collectors today whose eyes water for the same reason. A good Renaissance is now hard to procure, but a good Gothic is almost impossible.

To Raphael's cartoons is due the introduction of large figures in wide-curved draperies, also the half nude male figures with muscular anatomy as well defined as though directed by a physician. To him also is attributable a new series of Bible scenes in which large figures of men and women enact the life of Moses or of Solomon. At first these scenes took as background the Roman architecture, but soon the weavers fell back into old ways with the out-of-doors. Rome was far away, the Flemish landscape was a part of each man's consciousness, so back it came as a setting for Biblical scenes. The little hills with towered castles, the slopes all filled with rows of little puff-ball trees took the place of the arid lands of the Pharaohs and Judeans, and today we are glad of the childishness of the weaver.

Those who have had shown to them The Acts of the Apostles in the Vatican will remember the marvelous borders. Borders were a mere inconspicuous finish, a narrow frame, in Gothic work. In the Renaissance

204

tapestries they become a high type of design. The border on the plate which represents the Life of the Virgin illustrates the quiet fashion of the Gothic. That on the Garden Scene shows the change that the Renaissance introduced. The latter in its highest expression is an amazing result of fertile talent. The border is built up of scene after scene, each one of which might be used as subject for an entire tapestry. And interspersed with these are a hundred decorative motives from old carvings and paintings all intermixed with foliage, fruit and flowers.

In The Adoration of the Kings, which was woven at Brussels directly after the Raphael invasion, a man of talent has accomplished a marvel—he has retained the simplicity and purity of the older spirit, yet has released his figures from restraint. In other words has retained the spirit of the Gothic while introducing the technique of the more intellectual Renaissance. This background employs the ruins of old Rome, but without destroying the simplicity of atmosphere. And in the border he merely enlarges and amplifies the vegetation of preceding years.

Brussels retained her fame for many years. Although Bruges was an able second. The excellence of her production was not a matter of accident. Rules, severe ones, were established in the ateliers—I hesitate to call them factories though the great amount of their production would seem to class them as such. The master-weaver or chief of the atelier being of necessity an artist, had high ideals, and held his men to them. All were also members of the guilds, and thus came to an agreement as to standards of excellence.

A bewildering amount of orders poured into Brussels in this first half of the Sixteenth Century. All of Europe, and even beyond, began to feel that without tapestries the home of a noble or the palace of a king was notably incomplete. Orders before that century were apt to come for single pieces, often as gifts to the church. But after the Raphael set, the demand was for many. In the late Fifteenth Century one hanging held all the scenes of a history whether that history was of an individual or of a country's conquests. But Raphael's free drawings had set new fashions in this as well as in mannerisms of design. Each piece of tapestry thereafter must represent one scene only and many tapestries went to make up a set. The effect of this was to in-

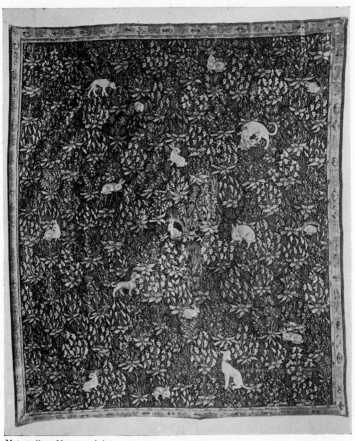

MILLEFLEURS TAPESTRY, ABOUT 1500. THE FLEMISH
TAPISSIER PICTURES HIS IMPRESSION OF THE FLOOR OF
THE SPRING FOREST

THE ADORATION OF THE KINGS.   BRUSSELS NEW MANNER IN 1525

crease the size of the orders. Fashion governs ever, and the fashion of sets in tapestries prevailed for two hundred years.

Perhaps it was pride, perhaps it was self-protection that caused the weavers of Brussels to enact a law that all their works which reached high standards of excellence should bear a certain mark woven into the galloon or tape with which the border of each piece was protected. This mark was formed by two affronted B's with a shield between, the two letters indicating the town of Brussels and the district of Brabant. Misuse of this symbol was forestalled by establishing most horrid penalties for the offender. Today we fall upon this mark with the joy of certain identification.

More than intriguing are some of the tapestries woven between 1518 and 1550. Usually one style dies by gradual decadence before another rises to splendor, and this causes a period of false art. But no such thing happened in Flanders tapestries. At the moment of the highest perfection of their Gothic manner, the ideals of the developed Renaissance were imposed upon the ateliers. And with high regard for the more intellectual ideals the mode was carefully copied.

But after a while an amusing thing happened, the tapissier drifted back into some of his old native ways. He became again a man who expressed in his art the peculiarities of his land and its people. And thus came tapestries which seemed like a transition between Gothic and Renaissance, but were really after the change instead of before it.

To this class belong many which delight those who revel in inconsistencies, such as an ostrich hunt where the hunters are dressed in Roman armor and the scene is set among the formal gardens of a Flemish castle. Many verdures were woven near the middle of the century, fascinating scenes of forest trees and flowers, with dogs and animals dashing about, and a distant background of hilly slopes with rows of tiny trees. They replace the millefleurs of Gothic times, but lack, alas, the exquisite naïveté of the earlier product.

Their borders are exponents of the newer manner, and altogether overbalance the central field by their sophistication, being composed of scenes and details purely Renaissance, and are woven with excess of width.

Sometimes two single figures like two persons from

Roman mythology or from Bible tales impose their conspicuous shapes upon such a verdure. And then one feels that in this the master of the atelier has woven only the figures. And apropos of the wide border, each atelier kept ready at hand many small drawings of figures and of ornamental details which the worker might combine at will. This type of verdure tapestry is one we often see and therefore is of interest.

Alas, we have to record the ultimate downfall of the Flemish tapestry. The pressure of orders led to unlovely cheapening of the work. Standards were lowered in designs, in weaving and in dyeing. Coarser threads make quicker results, so were adopted. Cheaper dyes and quicker methods of applying them were used. So the colors failed to stand the assaults of sunlight. It was a natural decay but a deplorable.

When the art revived it was in other countries and under the patronage of kings, but before reviewing those epochs a moment should be spent in glancing at Italy of the Sixteenth Century.

It was for some time her practise to impress the skill of Flanders into her service. The Raphael cartoons were sent to her more or less experimentally, to try out her ability. This being ably proved, more and yet more cartoons were dispatched to the famous weavers.

But Italy was not content. This was a time when the cities of northern Italy were peopled by conspicuous patrons of art. The Medici, the Sforza, the d'Este, the Tornabuoni families were among them. Add to these the popes, often supplied from the prominent families and it is easy to see that Italy might well ask why she should look outside for help in artistic matters.

The first step in weaving was to import into Italy certain talented tapissiers from Brussels, among them being Nicholas Karcher and John Rost. The former with his brother John were secured to superintend an experimental atelier by the Duke of Ferrara and the d'Este family. The cartoonist was of course Italian. The experiment succeeded in that atmosphere of Italy's high renaissance, and the work continued until the Duke's own large needs were supplied. Then followed a period of weaving for the public, and many a tapestry of exquisite perfection flowed out into Italian palaces. From 1534 to 1597 the ateliers flourished, and then the mode changed, the demand lessened, tapestries were no longer the most sought of decorative materials.

Andrea Mantegna must be mentioned as a cartoonist, and also Bacchiacca, as these two men were responsible for a type that has appeared in both of the high moments of tapestry weaving after the Gothic. This is the use of the so-called grotesques, small decorative figures found in Roman and Grecian art, such as the sphinx, the figure of man or boy which tapers off into acanthus leaves of a single point, or masks set in swags of fruit, caryatides, animals, and any other thing real or mythic. All this was drawn with no regard to natural scale, and all was lightly placed on a wide plain field of color. The Galleria degli Arrazzi in Florence shows examples to the interested wanderer. It was in the Eighteenth Century that this same type of composition was revived. The "triumphs" of the gods were also produced, figures from Olympus in small scale, each in its decorated niche. These were repeated in the Eighteenth Century.

Italy's tapestries, perfect as they were, with intelligence in the design and suavity in color, were only too few in number. They are scarcely obtainable now in these days when the finest examples are permanently enclosed in museums. The ateliers which came later grew a larger harvest, but for the tapestries they produced we have little love. They were the looms of the Barberini in the Seventeenth Century.

It was a time when art was affected by the followers of great masters of the past. Raphael had been succeeded by his florid pupil Guilio Romano, Rubens had appeared to carry exaggeration still further, and tapestries flaunted oversized figures unsuitable for hanging anywhere but in large public galleries or cathedrals. The two most perfect periods were entirely ended.

CHAPTER XIV

THE third great era of tapestry production. To Louis XIV is credited the flowering of the art. He established the Royal Manufactory of Furniture of the Crown in 1662 to 1667, and it took its name of the Gobelins from the private residence in which it was housed. At its formation it was intended for the manufacture of every sort of interior furnishing, but later became limited to the weaving of tapestries.

Behind this bald statement of a significant event in 1662, there is much of interest. Even the imperious Louis XIV could not have called into instant being this marvelously creative factory had there not been previous essays in the arts which he there assembled.

Turning a backward view we find that Francis I had concerned himself with an atelier for tapestries in France. Through all his life of change, of war, of imprisonment, or of flattering attention he had ever appreciated beauty. Being associated with all of Europe's rulers he strove to introduce into France whatever he saw of beauty outside. As he lived in the time when the Renaissance was sweeping over Europe, scattering its seeds on each country in turn, it was but natural that he should gratify ambition by setting tasks for his own people, teaching them new ways in decoration. Tapestries being then a necessity of kings and nobles as well as of prosperous merchants, he obtained satisfaction by establishing high-warp looms in the palace of which he was so fond, the wooded domain of Fontainebleau.

It was short-lived, this factory, but there is one set woven here which all may see for it hangs at the museum connected with the Gobelins in Paris. It is called the History of Diana, and knowing the fondness of the King for Diane de Poitiers a bit of romance is disassociable from the hanging.

After Francis' death Catherine de' Medici kept occupied the looms for her own gratification, but her husband Henry II ran to Paris with his ambitions and made a sort of charity or social-service work of tapestry weaving. He had looms set up in the Hospital of La Trinité, an orphan asylum, and had the children trained in weaving. Two things make this venture of interest, one was the weaving a few years later of a set drawn in the florid manner of Giulio Romano which was called the History of Mausolus and Artemisia. The heroine was intended to represent Catherine de' Medici in the luxury of woe as widow. The other note of interest is that this same tapestry factory of La Trinité was one of the group gathered together to form the Gobelins.

Still looking for the germs of the industry that assumed such importance under Louis XIV, one falls upon the picturesque figures of Henri IV, that great king of Navarre who came to the throne by such a narrow margin of chance, a chance that was furthered by the death, encouraged or natural, of three other heirs.

It was he who threw out over France the Edict of Nantes which was to stop the steady persecution of Protestants which had grown insupportable and all in the name of religion. By the relief gained through this famous Edict, France recovered those of her weavers who had fled to other countries, for the French are never entirely happy out of France.

Weavers came also from Flanders, and thus Henri had at once the material needed for establishing tapestry looms in Paris. He began as early as 1597, having then been reigning but eight years. And here he invited Maurice du Bourg the most talented tapissier who was educated at the old orphanage factory of La Trinité.

Soon he had the Flemish weavers of Paris in his employ with their renowned masters François de la Planche and Marc Comans. In this he was fortunate for these men had proved their ability by conducting their factories as profitable business enterprises, and even establishing ateliers at Tours and at Amiens. It was they who helped James I of England to establish the Mortlake factory.

It was because the tapestry factories were always private enterprises that the art lived precariously, for rarely is the artist a business man. Henri IV was the first monarch to realize that the State should assume the financial responsibility and leave the artist and artist weaver unembarrassed by the need of funds. Notwithstanding the contentions of his prime minister Sully that agriculture was the salvation of France and the arts were questionable luxuries, Henri established a tapestry factory in the Tuileries with Du Bourg about 1607 and that also was one of the group which Louis XIV gathered together to form the Gobelins. It had the distinction of being the first tapestry factory owned and operated by the State. There was also another as famous known as Les Tournelles in honor of the district where it was first established, though it changed its name with its habitat when moved to the Faubourg St. Marceau.

In all, the king, Henri IV, supported five tapestry works in Paris. But except that they were all occupied in producing fine hangings there was no unity among them. It took the autocratic mind of Louis XIV to pick them all up like scattered bits and bind them together in one cooperative whole. But let us not forget in giving him the glory that the paternal Henri of Navarre had indicated the way.

For a clue to the style of tapestry that led up to what is called confusingly the French Renaissance it should be remembered that Greco-Roman styles of the true Renaissance had still a preeminent place in art. They were however enfeebled by constant copying with no new elements introduced. It seemed impossible for an artist to draw a fine design without giving the restraint of the Greco-Roman. The loosening of this mode was the task of artists not yet on the field. We are able to find an occasional tapestry of the factories of Henri IV, and see it holding to the old traditions making no attempt at introducing innovations.

Coming a little nearer to the time of the establishment of the Gobelins, the factory at Maincy north of Paris is discovered, and this if one reads between the lines of historic fact, would seem to have had a large influence in developing the desire of Louis XIV to reign over factories of his own. It was the factory belonging to Nicolas Foucquet, Superintendent of Finance. This resplendent and ambitious gentleman established and maintained a tapestry factory the products of which were for himself alone, for the decoration of the great salons at Vaux and to make regal gifts where such gifts were advantageous.

The factory, established in 1658, lasted but three or four years, but in that time attained importance. It is here we hear of Le Brun as chief cartoonist, Le Brun the greatest decorative artist of France, he who was

218

called to be the head of the Gobelins. The Hunt of Meleager now on view in Paris at the Gobelins was one of his works while master at Foucquet's private factory.

Foucquet was accused of diverting public funds. His tapestry looms were taken to Paris and blended with the ever-accumulating foundation stones of the Gobelins. His weavers, Flemish all, were taken over by the crown and Le Brun, the great Le Brun went to Paris as first artist of the Court. Colbert took then the office of the obliterated Foucquet and stood beside the king and state ever after.

CHAPTER XV

TO establish dates for the Gobelins factory, known as Le Manufacture Royal des Meubles de la Couronne, let us regard the tablets secured to the walls at the present day although little regarded by the usual visitor to the uninspiring industry of today. The first tells us that Jean and Philibert Gobelin, merchant dyers in scarlet and who have left their name to this quarter of Paris, and to the manufacture of tapestries, had here their atelier on the banks of the Bièvre at the end of the Fifteenth Century.

The second states that in April 1601 Marc Comans and François de la Planche, Flemish tapestry weavers installed their ateliers on the banks of the Bièvre. The next date named is September 1667 when Colbert established in the buildings of the Gobelins the manufacture of furnishings for the Crown under the directions of Charles Le Brun.

It was Le Brun who instituted a style distinctly of

France by breaking away from diluted styles of the Renaissance and discovering a more natural mode of expression. The style was grandiose, but so was the spirit of the King for whom the style was evolved. We may not like its too abundant masses, its pompousness, its lack of the common human touch. But the style in its first years should be considered not as a high period of art, but rather as a new movement on which a more pleasing art was formed. In this light it can only be considered as of ultra importance to France which from this time to the end of the Eighteenth Century led the world of decoration.

The earlier tapestries of the Gobelins were scenes of ancient conquest and triumph, for the King ever thought himself a parallel to Alexander the Great or one of the Cæsars. Sometimes the scene was modern with Louis as the dominant figure, his small stature skilfully magnified by high heels, voluminous coat and preposterous wig. These hangings were of enormous size for large rooms were the mode. Later there were compositions illustrating winemaking or some other occupation of the people dominated by the classic god or goddess appropriate to the occasion—Ceres for the harvest, Pomona or Bacchus for the vine.

Notwithstanding the frequent scenes wherein the myths of Olympus enact their traditions, the method of portral changed utterly from the manner of the Renaissance. The goddesses might well be women of the court at Versailles, so realistic are they, arrayed in jewels and costumes suggestive of the day's mode. An essay was made at tapestries which were entirely located on Olympus, nothing of France about them, and as usual the gods were displayed in frank nudity. During the dominance of the ostensibly pious and modest Madame de Maintenon this was discontinued at her command. She even had completed tapestries of this sort returned to the loom to be dressed with much yardage of heavy drapery. This accounts for the hidden outlines of Psyche, of Hebe and other adolescent beauties who then were lost in ballooning folds.

But as the art of France progressed, these errors passed like a discarded mode, and there grew a greater refinement, a stronger intellectual appeal. A series of Royal Residences is illustrative of this. Earlier the

BRUSSELS TAPESTRY, 1550. ITALIAN GROTESQUES

TAPESTRY FROM ATELIERS OF HENRI IV, 1601. BATTLE OF
THE SABINES. STRONG EVIDENCE OF ITALIAN RENAISSANCE

mode would have been to occupy the greater part of the tapestry with a palace or château. But with the increasing refinement of the advancing art the architectural gem is placed in the far distance, giving reason for a smaller scale, and all the rest of the picture is occupied with an entourage of garden detail through the shady trees of which the far distant royal residence shines brightly in the sunlight.

One more style of design must be noted because of its effect upon French art as it developed into the bewitching styles of the Eighteenth Century, for it is not all at once that a style crystallizes. Design does not spring full-armed into being like Pallas from the head of Jove, but is a growth, or if you like, a mounting of steps. There was then a fashion that ran parallel to the self-conscious sumptuous mode of the Louis XIV style in tapestries. It was the liberal use of grotesques as drawn by the talented master Jean Bérain. By the word is not meant caricatures or deformation, but those exquisite fancies of the artists of Greece and Rome and of the Renaissance. They serve as detail in borders of Raphael tapestries. Indeed they are but small details, yet Bérain's talent could fill with these small objects an entire field. He could build them up into a composition as exquisite and satisfying as a scene composed of human forms.

He became the mode. He was copied all over Europe. His grotesques met the eye in every salon for they were used as wall and ceiling decorations. They even went to Lyons as designs for weavers and were thus translated into silks of the period. It took but the introduction of Chinese eccentric curves to turn them into suitable motives for the rococo of Asiatic inspirations in the style Louis XV. Those who contributed to the development of French art at the end of the Seventeenth Century were the far-seeing artists who questioned the preceding ideals, who selected from among the new, who eliminated, and who modified, and thus a new and distinct style was evolved for France. Its three phases are well known and named for the three kings called Louis.

To return a moment to Colbert the able director, the power behind the throne, he held ever a strong interest in textiles and built up for France an enormous trade in them. To this end he formed a weaver's code which compelled perfection. No inferior fabrics were allowed to issue from the looms.

Tapestries being the highest product of weaving it was but consistent that he should be ambitious to have the tapestries of France superior to all others, as Arras and Brussels tapestries had once been. When the factory called the Gobelins was started the weaving of tapestries was but one of its arts. It was only in later years that it was devoted exclusively to the high-warp looms. It therefore seemed insufficient to the ambitious Colbert who then inaugurated other centers of production. The Beauvais works were founded in 1664. To these we look for the smooth fine furniture coverings in the next reign. In 1665 he caught up Aubusson, shook from it the dust of its ancient history, infused it with new blood, and gave it a prominent place as a new venture. All three of these factories were named as belonging to the crown, and all were in fact supported by the State. Colbert's great genius was supplemented by the coffers of France into which his hands were allowed to dig deeply by permission of the King.

This matter of crown support was the great stroke of

genius that developed the art of France. It gave her the position of creator in art, by the simple though costly experiment of freeing the men of talent from the necessity of finding money for daily living. Money was lavishly spent on them, they were given apartments in the Louvre, they saw their works adorn palaces. With this encouragement art developed into the beauties of the Eighteenth Century.

Louis XIV gave one great check to the weavers, both those of the high-warp tapestry and those humbler ones of Lyons and the cloth-producing towns. Deceived as to the status of Protestantism in France he repealed the Edict of Nantes. The effect was deplorable and instantaneous. Protestant artists and workers fled the country for their lives. England then gained such designers as Daniel Marot who paused by way of Holland, and such Lyonese weavers of silk as established in London the Spitalfields looms still existing. As England had been a large market for Lyons silks this re-action injured French trade while it forced on England an advantage she might never have had if foreign silk weavers had not come in numbers to teach her hand new and adept ways.

BRUSSELS TAPESTRY, SIXTEENTH CENTURY, REPRESENTING
ONE OF A SERIES OF THE MONTHS BY BERNARD VAN ORLEY

It is impossible to separate styles in the Eighteenth Century with as neat a date as that which separates the reigns of kings. It was during the entire first half of the century that the style called after Louis XV matured and came to full flowering. Bérain and Audran, Oudry, Watteau, Boucher, all contributed their amazing talent. The system being continued of state support of artists, work went on at the Gobelins, and at this time were executed marvelous tapestries. Colbert was no more, Le Brun was dead, but the Gobelins after various vicissitudes was ably directed by Jules de Cotte from 1699 to 1735.

We have to note the Don Quixote series of twenty-eight pieces, even though the opportunity to see an example is rare. Mr. Joseph Widener has part of a magnificent set with cramosie, or crimson, background brought to America by Mr. Pierpont Morgan. Mr. Clarence Mackay has a part set of lighter more neutral color brought here by the late Mrs. John W. Mackay. In England the Duchess of Rutland possesses a few pieces. To describe them sketchily, the scenes from the great romance of the knight are drawn by Charles Coypel, and are in small scale in the center of the tapestry, while the greater space of the hanging is filled with decorative matter that has never been surpassed in the assembling, a wide field of color in two tones lying between the smallish picture and the decoration. This decoration is the quintessence of delicacy, of naturalism combined with fantasy, and illustrates the perfection of an art that was truly French. Although this famous set was composed in the time of Louis XIV, it is illustrative of the style attributed to his successor, showing how early that style began its development.

We should remember that while Coypel drew the cartoons, Audran and Lemaire composed the surrounding decoration in which centers most of the interest. Also that the artists' work would have been marred had the weavers not been men of high talent. Their work is indicative of the times when unreason of design is forgiven for the perfection of technical execution.

The style *rocaille,* or rococo, which flashes all through the reign of Louis XV is but little seen in tapestries. The hangings in the middle of the century were still hung loosely on the wall, and were better ornament for the rooms and background of the frivolous life led within them when dealing with large scenes of mythology. But the borders give the clue to the tendency of the moment. They had shrunk from the wide border of exquisite Renaissance personages and that later one of overgrown fruit and scroll, to a clever copying of a gilded frame. It is in the detail of this frame that one finds the ornament popular until tapestry borders ceased altogether.

And the reason for their ceasing? The very simple one that the proper tapestry of the ages past was no longer the fashion. They were torn down from the walls and auctioned off with furniture which was no longer of the mode, and thus found their way into the homes of unfashionable folk. The mode was for smaller rooms with paneled walls and much woodwork. So the tapestries were asked to reduce themselves to the size of these small panels, the carved border of which served as border for the tapestry.

It was the imperious whim of du Barry which introduced the figure of a negro into tapestry cartoons. From afar came a waif, a small black child from Burma the almost unknown Asia. Zamora he was called, and she made of him a pet, as of an exceptionally intelligent monkey. He could speak only with his eyes and smile, but she kept him near her radiant person at fêtes and receptions, for his dark skin contrasted piquantly with hers which was of snow and roses. She wore him as an accessory to her toilette, one might say, and gave him the privileges sometimes accorded a lap-dog.

But Zamora passed the age of holding parasols over his mistress, and when her power fell he joined those who robbed her retreat of "Louveciennes," and aided all he could to throw her to the mob who eventually sent her to the guillotine a few months after the decapitation of the King, Louis XVI. But he was the negro as a motive in decorative drawing.

Before the time of reduction in size many hangings had been made. There was a series of the Hunts of Louis XV showing the monarch slim and youthful, smartly arrayed, and elegantly posed in a charming stretch of woodland with *allées* leading to distant enchantment. Almost a verdure tapestry it seems, and in strong contrast to the "History of the King," executed for Louis XIV where he ever appears as the self-centered monarch but also as the head of a great national movement or interest of state.

The young Madame de Pompadour flashed piquantly through those woods where Louis XV was portrayed as huntsman. From that time on she may be called the Queen of the Gobelins factory. As she had a passion for accumulating houses, and a strong decorative instinct coupled with the courtesan's disregard of expense, the works were ever busy with her commands.

Such men as Oeben and Caffieri supplied her with furniture and bronze ornament. Such men as the Coypels drew tapestry cartoons. The Gobelins factory executed all, and the state paid the bills—but with ever increasing dissatisfaction. This was the time when Boucher was creating a world of amorini, pink fleshed and piquant, ever gamboling in clouds, but with a sophistication not given to infants born away from the influence of a false gay court. These were sprinkled into scenes which were named for the gods, scenes in which the personages looked suspiciously like court beauties taking advantage of their mythological pseudonyms to frolic in questionable ways.

The greatest change in the tapestries of this time was

231

in this, that whereas in former times they were decorative hangings of a limited color scale, they now became paintings in silk and wool. This necessitated an enormous increase in the number of colors necessary to the tapissier. If he must depict the flush on Chloe's cheek, and the olive skin of her lover, there must be threads of a thousand tints for the portrayal. And so from the Gothic scale of fifteen or twenty colors with which to weave magic, we come by hasty increase to twenty thousand. The matter to be deplored in this connection is that with these fine graduations of tones the sun plays tricks. Such subtle distinctions and shadings were made that the slightest fading of the colors altered them. Thus much of the original tender beauty is gone from the finest tapestries of the reign of the Pompadour.

Verdures of the Eighteenth Century must not be forgotten. They were composed with the skill of him who loves the forest, who like the Chinese painter ruminates for days among green trees, studies flowers and yields to bird-enchantment. Going to his studio full of the spirit of the wood he records impressions with inspired hands. If he is truly inspired he sketches in blue-greens rather than in yellow-greens, and re-places the modest birds of the home woodland with gorgeous parrots or mackaws.

Styles changed again with Louis XVI, but they cast their shadow before. The Pompadour in spite of her talents, her steady head, her political ability, in spite of her resources in entertaining a dull and weary king, she was deposed, and du Barry reigned in her stead until the King's death in 1774. Although she too used lavishly the tapestries of France, she had a more modest wish in regard to the number of resi-dences than had du Barry. Her influence on the change in style was less than that of the young Dau-phiness Marie Antoinette for whom the classicism that followed was in part adopted.

In a reign dominated by the two great courtesans La Pompadour and du Barry, able though they were, it is refreshing to think upon the advent of a new influence, one simpler, cleaner, if less inspired than its predecessor. The marriage of the grandson of Louis XV to Marie Antoinette necessitated notice in the world of decoration and as Louis XV died but four years after this mating, the style introduced for the

Dauphiness was taken as the keynote for the style named for the new King Louis XVI. It was inspired by those liberal excavations at Pompeii which were then proceeding with enthusiasm. From this Greco-Roman gem was drawn the designs of the new mode. It was the same old source—Italy.

The classic was revived in tapestries and there came from the looms of the Gobelins some sets which pictured the Olympian gods in a purely classic way. These tapestries though formal were exquisite, and though innumerable figures were treated were never crowded as the personages were ranged in rows, each with its niche or pedestal and its symbols, a delightful presentation of mythology. Only the manual adroitness of the long-trained weavers were capable of executing such designs.

But, alas, the day of tapestries was finished. The inspired work of a century of brilliant production was over. Just as Gothic tapestries after reaching bewildering beauty were blotted out, and as the intellectual perfection of the high Renaissance was overcome by loose methods of artists and weavers, so this last great period of tapestry weaving, the Eighteenth Century

TAPESTRY OF LATE SEVENTEENTH CENTURY, LOUIS XIV PERIOD,
POMONA

BEAUVAIS TAPESTRY, SIGNED FRANÇOIS BOUCHER, 1757

fell before the fickleness of fashion aided by conditions in the political world.

The fashion was for smaller rooms than those in which the tapestries of twenty to thirty feet in length had been extended. Not only that but the walls were so decorated with paneling of carved wood that tapestry was no longer a necessity. Men from the royal factories executed the exquisite *boiserie* that filled all decorative needs. So tapestries grew smaller and ever smaller. It is enough to illustrate their change in decorative importance to remember that the exquisite hangings of the classic type described above were used only as protection from the draughts of doorways, and were humbly named the "Portières des Dieux."

Some charming bits are left us of simple composition and high color, children or young peasants of high sophistication playing at rustic tasks. These were woven without border, for filling in the panels of painted rooms where the woodwork consisted of moldings, not of carvings. Incidentally these bright rectangular pieces which are not fragments but complete in themselves are delightfully sympathetic with our Twentieth Century habitations.

At last they vanished from the wall, the woven pictures, and sank to the level of coverings for furniture. Marie Antoinette with her love of simulating the simple and bucolic life, favored the designs that illustrated the Fables of La Fontaine. Full of animals, birds, peasants, these simple subjects pleased her in her hours at the Trianon and at the Hameau where she played at dairy-maid.

Another favorite subject for furniture coverings was the history of Don Quixote, but not fit to be compared in design or execution to the great set of Audran and Coypel woven by Cozette and other men of talent. Other coverings, purely decorative and carrying no story were the exquisite scrolls of the acanthus —the rinceau—combined with dainty flowers.

At this time the factory at Aubusson was furnishing many of the floor-coverings. To Beauvais was confided the execution of the furniture coverings, which were woven on low-warp looms. At Beauvais also were woven many of the Boucher hangings. Both factories it will be remembered were under the patronage of the State, which supplied the funds.

The last note one can record in old tapestries is the

brief revival in Beauvais tapestry furniture coverings after the rise of Napoleon as Emperor. These in execution were as fine as any ever woven by that factory, perhaps even finer than any other furniture coverings. In design they copied antique vessels and amphoræ with much use of Roman medallions in the borders.

With this last bright flash the art of tapestry making lapsed.

And today? This is not a time when the weaving of tapestries is an impulsive expression of art. It is a time of the strongest appreciation of the work of the artists and weavings of other days. We acquire but we do not create.

Highest in our present appreciation stands the Gothic in its best moment. There is scarcely an interior which is not appropriately decorated by the marvelous creations in silk, wool and gold of this greatest of all tapestry periods. But they are practically unobtainable, all having found permanent haven in museums and in great collections which will become the property of museums.

Next we love the Renaissance with its skilfully drawn pictures, its fascinating verdures and its borders born of erudition. These suit our greater houses and can still be found to the infinite satisfaction of those who can acquire. Indeed I can scarcely think of a large country house of great hall and generous rooms as complete without one.

The third great period of tapestries, the Eighteenth Century, gives innumerable alluring pieces, of not too large a size, and on these we fall with delight. The best examples of the times for a century after the establishment of the Gobelins are exceedingly rare, but those of lesser quality have great charm and with it the qualities that make them appropriate to Twentieth Century homes.

Each age had its bad examples, hangings made of poor materials by clumsy workmen. There are no bad tapestries, only some are better than others, is the shibboleth of the enthusiast.

The factory at Aubusson, notwithstanding its claims of long descent, put out acres and acres of coarse verdures, and in this purely commercial effort forgot all traditions of art and conscientious weaving. In one of those fascinating hunts for the antique which take one through the labyrinth of the Latin Quarter,

BEAUVAIS TAPESTRY BY BOUCHER, 1754, WOVEN BY OUDRY

INDIAN DESIGN, SEVENTEENTH OR EIGHTEENTH CEN-
TURY, EXECUTED IN RESIST-DYE AND PAINTING

these are almost all the small dealer has to offer, and they are usually in fragments. On this rough diet must the appetite for tapestries most frequently be fed, although a scrap of Renaissance verdure may sometimes be had.

Yet for all our distaste of poor dull color, rough wool and bad weaving, we seize these bits with eagerness because with them we can give an air of elegance and distinction to our rooms by covering with them chairs of ancient make and cushions for sofa or floor. In these days old tapestries are used down to the last scrap, for the supply is almost exhausted.

It would seem that hanging a tapestry in a modern home required no imagination whatever, merely a workman who could mount a step-ladder. But there is a word of reminder—tapestries were not made to lie too flat against the wall. A little looseness, not actual folds but an easing, adds charm. This suggestion is perhaps unwelcome to one who has paid extravagantly for a tapestry. Let him try it both ways then, stretched flat like a painting, or elegantly easy, and he is sure to like the latter way better. Small pieces and fragments must perforce hang like any narrow ornamental textile.

In the Fifteenth and Sixteenth Centuries a lord's tapestries were suspended from great hooks. That method becomes well the stone or rough-plastered room or hall of today, especially if the hooks are made a matter of ornament, finished with an iron fleur-de-lis, for example. The effect is more than harmonious, it is one of those little matters which help to give the proper atmosphere to a room of old-world fashion.

If no mention has been made of tapestry looms outside of Arras, Brussels, Paris, France, and Italy, it is only because we have reviewed but the three high points of tapestry history, and the three great centers of production. Most of the cheaper tapestries obtainable today which are not a poor quality of Aubusson, come from these outside factories, and but for the scarcity of good hangings would never receive the attention that now is theirs.

CHAPTER XVI

PRINTED COTTON AND LINEN

THERE is a story even in chintz, or what we ordinarily call cretonne. It forms a chapter in the great romance of navigation and discovery, and sets one on board of the early cargo ships "floating through the tropics by the palm-green shores," as Masefield dreams.

The first printed cottons in Europe came from the fertile East. One comes at last to feel that every textile and every fundamental design originated in either Near East or Far East. The sagacity of Europe lies in her recognizing the beauty of the Oriental ornament and of commercializing it, to the end that many may share that beauty, and that trade may lead to prosperity of the nations.

Recall then the first adventurous men who dared push their small ships into the unknown, for month after month of suspense, until a passage was found to India; and those later adventurers following the established route who attached portions of Eastern countries to their own by force or craft "in the name of the Crown." Then center the memory on the ambitions of Holland, France and England, all three of which in the Seventeenth Century formed commercial bodies named East India Companies. A generous salt of adventure goes with their experiences. Government owned were these new businesses which gave their personnel an official carriage, not conquest in their minds perhaps, not war exactly, but a firm and gentleman-like encroachment for the sake of civilization—meaning landing-places, warehouses and the like, for trade.

Thus it came that England possessed herself of Madras, and France of Pondicherry, both in the province of Coromandel on the Eastern coast of southern India. Of course they came to disagreements born of rivalry, the British East India Company and the French East India Company, and war in 1744 put Madras in the hands of the French. But it was less than thirty years after, that British power over India had so extended that Warren Hastings was named as the first governor-general in 1772.

These are the historic facts, but the lesser ones are of more interest to our study, the journeys of the cargo ships and the goods with which they filled their holds for the return journey and which were sold to merchants in France and England. In the Seventeenth and Eighteenth Centuries they brought cotton prints.

Behind that simple statement there lie many details. First, the prints they brought were of surpassing beauty. They were not, as now, quickly made factory productions, but were veritable works of art. Women of the Eighteenth Century had the trained taste of those who live in luxurious surroundings. It was a century of beauty in all the arts, and these discriminating women made chintz the fashion.

The painted cloths from India were rich in color, and full of ancient tradition in design. The manner of making them was intricate, requiring not only talent but infinite patience and the employment of several arts. And these charming exotics that were spread before those lovely ladies of Europe in the Seventeenth and Eighteenth Century, are the ancestors of the mountains of chintz that fill our shops today.

Palampores, or bed covers, they called the oblongs

from India, and at this time the most favored design for these was the Tree of Life, a straying meander of slender branches all aflower with blooms of many kinds, the tree-trunk small and planted in a pyramid of rocks. But its exquisite tones and shades were impossible to describe, also the symbolism of the border which reaches back to far antiquity.

Of course these cloths were promptly seized and laid upon the mahogany bed of the day as a coverlet, or hung on the wall behind the bed's head and elsewhere. Their price was too high for all the hangings of a bed, so the valance, tester and curtains were often of other material. And what went so well with the new Asiatic chintz as Turkey-red cloth, which also was an imported fabric. The traveler of today who lunches at a certain hotel in Fontainebleau can lounge in a library there decorated with this same combination of India print and red calico and fancy the Eighteenth Century returned.

In those old times the chintz was lined, not left to float unprotected, and strangely enough it was lined with a woolen fabric called moreen which resembles a coarse moiré silk. This suggests the state of Europe in

244

regard to cotton. Strange it seems to us that cotton was a rarity, that cotton goods could cost more than silk, linen, or wool.

The ships brought cotton to Europe, but already woven, not as cotton wool. The astonishment was great to find that cotton grew on a plant as a fruit, and was not the plant itself as in the case of hemp or flax—and that it would not grow in France or England.

Wherever the demand is great, commerce and industry busy themselves. The price of a palampore being high, as much as a hundred and fifty dollars for one of great beauty, and the public being clamorous for something cheaper, manufacturers experimented with weaves and dyes, and at last produced a printed cotton cloth in which laborious processes were replaced by simple mechanical expedients.

Thus it came that all France and all England flowered like a June garden, and the cottage interior became as gay as madame's boudoir. All honor to the venturesome little ships that sailed East and brought home a beauty which inspired the development of one of the world's greatest industries. Silk had furnished houses and dressed the persons of the rich for centuries, but home-spun linen and wool had been the apparel of the cottager, tight woven and dark dyed that it might stand all endurance tests. We can imagine then the joy with which a humble class fell upon a gay be-flowered textile, costing little but which enlivened the somber cottage and made of every woman a figure of light.

Before this happy condition was reached, much water flowed under the mill-wheel. When importations from India became heavy, the crown in England feared for home industries, and tried by taxation to reduce the incoming flood. But the lady of the draw-ing-room evaded laws or overstepped her income, for the fashion of painted or printed cottons was her obsession. These things suited the furniture of the day which was mostly of mahogany and needed viv-ifying.

After much experimenting England imported India's raw cotton and wove her own cotton cloth and learned how to print gay designs thereon. Then her produc-tion became so great that weavers of silk and wool raised hands of objection to the Government, protesting against the ruining of their business. Odd it seems now, almost absurd, but then a trade tragedy. The plea was regarded as reasonable, and a heavy tax was put on domestic printed cottons.

But even that could not stop the progress though we hear of indignant weavers tearing printed frocks from the shoulders of ladies who ventured into factory districts wearing the proscribed fabric, and of officers of the law even seizing the India hangings of David Garrick's bed.

By gradual improvements supplied by an enthusiast here, a mechanic there, printing by engraved plates was invented and the cylinder method of printing was developed. Until the second half of the Eighteenth Century European printing on textiles was done with wooden blocks, a sort of stamping, involving the labor of lifting and replacing the block many times to print a yard of goods. The newer method had the pattern engraved on a large cylinder which passed over the cloth in endless revolutions, leaving behind its patterned track.

That this mechanical producing compares with the wondrous handmade prints of India, it were absurd to contend. But the ultimate result of this invention is

247

the mass production of our time which fills a need of our day.

The process of making the Indian palampore, or any other dyed and painted cloth brought to Europe in the Seventeenth and Eighteenth Centuries, is one so long and technical that a detailed description would be a weariness to read unless the reader is a student of dyeing. Let it suffice to remember but a few points which influenced European makers of printed cloths. The fabric was a fine cotton, cotton being a rare tissue in Europe until the demand for printed stuffs arose. The length of cloth was first treated to a bath of some slightly oily fluid, beaten and stretched. The design was outlined and then various mordants were applied to certain parts, and melted wax to others. When the cloth thus prepared was dipped into a dye of a single color, a variety of colors were developed by contact with the various mordants, and spaces covered with wax (resist dye so-called) had no color at all when the wax was removed. After this the brush was used, dipped in reliable pigments, and the design was thus completed. But this slight explanation gives no account of the number of times the cloth is dipped and dried, nor of the painstaking task of painting finest details, nor of the skilled preparation of the colors, nor of the months of close application to the work required for the making of a hanging or a coverlet.

Only in the Orient are such works of steady patience possible. Other countries than India have similar processes. Old records speak of "Java Belts" which probably mean the same batiks that Java has made for centuries, but is like to stop making if Manchester continues the work of factory-made copies. The Java process is very like the Indian, a long painstaking system, women sitting three or four months over a single cloth for ten or twelve hours a day. Siamese cloths also are mentioned among old importations. It will be remembered that Louis XIV threw a hand to the Orient and plucked from Ayuthia in Siam a strange ambassador to France, and his company it was that brought the native printed or painted cloth decorated with stripes and squares, still worn by Siamese.

In France as in England the first imported cottons from India arrived in the second half of the Seventeenth Century and awakened at once the desire for possession in the breast of every person of wealth or social consequence. The more they bought, the more the returning ships brought to them. And the greater the consumption of this artistic novelty, the less was the demand for French silks and woolens.

It became therefore the pleasure and duty of domestic print weavers to protest, and of the State to pass laws of prohibition. Between 1686 and 1750 no less than thirty decrees were issued in France in restraint of the use of printed cottons. But prohibition fails to exclude. There is a naughtiness in human nature, a half-humorous rebellion that makes us snatch at things denied. All the well planned restrictions of France failed to abolish the use of printed cottons.

Indian prints were ever very high in price. All who appreciated could not afford them. Thus it came that French textile workers set about making an imitation to sell at low cost.

Their first efforts employed the wood-block, dipped in color, placed on the goods, given a stroke of the hammer, the block removed and the process repeated. Slow and inadequate the method was, and results when compared with the Indian palampore were pitiably poor. Relief comes when labor is too great. In France as in England two new processes were invented, printing from copper plates on which designs of great beauty and delicacy could be engraved, and printing from cylinders which rolled the pattern in endless repeating while the goods passed between. Home production was at last in position to supply all demands, and even to export to other countries. Then the weavers of silk, wool, and linen wept afresh, for these prolific factories seemed a menace to their market.

Another reason this for laws and prohibitions, another reason then for fashionables laughingly to flout the law. Fancy the glee with which La Pompadour must have arranged a suite of rooms in "Bellevue" one of her many country houses. She hung the walls, she curtained the windows, she draped the bed, and covered the chairs, with as many yards of printed stuff as could be employed. And this was probably as much from *mechanceté* as from appreciation of the fashionable new fabric, for the very Crown which paid her bills was the same that signed prohibitory decrees making unlawful her pretty indulgence.

A deeper interest clings to the French product called toile de Jouy than to any other European decorative prints. There is reason in this interest for the tale of the factory and its master includes great persons and great political movements. And quite apart from these the Jouy prints themselves are of a beauty that ever appeals, the artistic expression of the Eighteenth Century. Their designs suggest a world of insouciance in which we can live in day-dreams, groups of personages dancing in gipsy scenes, or picnicking al fresco, couples alone on scrappy little islands where none may observe the subtleties of their love game, pagodas lightly floating on a ragged bit of earth attached to heaven by scrolls and flower-chains. These and a thousand more delicious fancies charm us as they charmed the people of long ago. Well for us of these hasty unreflecting days if we have about us some of these provocative prints to set us dreaming. The Jouy prints best represent the printed work of France. Although they seemed to us to have sprung into being without a gradual process of perfecting, much labor went before, and much conflict between trade and fashion.

It was in 1759 that the manufacturing at Jouy was established. This statement might lead one to think of large buildings of a great industry. The start was modest enough. Its housing was in a small cottage, where its founder worked alone. His first length of printed goods was delivered in 1760, and for this work he had himself been designer, engraver and printer.

Christophe Philippe Oberkampf's history is the history of toile de Jouy. He was a little boy in his native duchy of Württemberg when he was apprenticed to a dyer. He was but twenty when he founded the factory at Jouy, the village near Versailles through which many of us pass unaware in these days of motor tours.

This was officially in 1759 although he had been at work in other places making successful *indiennes* as the prints were then called. A petty official of the State, the Guardian of Financial Archives, having learned ahead of time that at last all legal restrictions on printed cloths were to be removed in 1759, thought to make a little business advantage for himself. He hastily set up a factory, and knowing of Oberkampf's ability offered to him the entire management of this factory. From this small beginning grew the great works which supplied a French public avid for the artistic prints and which were exported to other countries as well.

A change in the process of printing with engraved

copper-plates made in 1770 was the cause of the production of prints all in one color, the soft colors of mauve, puce, blue, red, which nowadays it is such a pleasure to find. The look of the old Indian fabrics disappeared and French designs took their place, largely they were scenes, fanciful scenes of joyous living, whether among fashionable folk or among rustics. To complete the pattern these scenes were connected by a scheme of filling spaces with pure decoration.

Oberkampf himself will never be forgotten in the industrial annals of France. His relations with his workers were ideal. He lived in a house at the gate of the factory enclosure and made of himself a just master and friend to all. The bell with which the employees were called to work and released as well, was rung by his own hands, and this little item of his history is lovingly preserved.

The Revolution came. With reluctance Oberkampf saw his laborers disappear, but it was not for long. He prepared for a revival by buying all the imported cotton cloth that was available to print when peace should be restored. Money, the paper bills of those troubled times, depreciated day by day, but the cotton goods

INDIAN PALAMPORE, PAINTED, SEVENTEENTH CEN-
TURY. TREE OF LIFE

INDIAN PAINTED COTTON, SEVENTEENTH CENTURY. SCENES FROM LIFE held their value. Thus he argued. He was printing large designs when the upheaval came, designs for the royal châteaux. Groups of personages both real and allegorical spoke loyalty to kings and nobles. Oberkampf by clever juggling with the plates gave them a twist toward the newer trend of public thought and made them signify the triumph of the Republic. A lettered ribbon, a descriptive title, altered many a drawing that otherwise would have brought disaster to the Jouy factory.

In 1806, the Emperor and Empress, Napoleon and Josephine, one day surprised Oberkampf with a visit to the factory, nor did Napoleon fail to ask a thousand questions after his usual manner. So pleased was the Emperor that he made of Oberkampf a member of the Legion of Honor, supplying him with the decoration which he detached from his own coat. Napoleon came again—this time with the new Empress, Marie Louise.

Artists for designs at the end of the century, were the same as those able draughtsmen who worked for silk factories. But one can fancy them designing with far greater enthusiasm for the Jouy factory. There are technical difficulties in relation to woven representations, but almost none to printing, especially after the introduction of copper plates and cylinder printing. Exactly as a man drew his scenes they might be etched on the copper. Thus came such beautiful cloths as those which show the designs of Jean Baptiste Huet.

Huet's talent belonged entirely to the art of the diminutive, an art that rejoiced in detail, or rather in the portrayal of an infinite number of persons and animals small in scale. He had the gift of infusing these with a vitality that even the classic drawings missed. His invention was without limit and fancies flowed easily from his delicate brush.

He is perhaps most loved for his portrayal of animals. Whatever the subject of his plate might be he never failed to introduce into it a few active little creatures, and usually those of a homely nature like ducks or doves, goats or lambs, and his ever present dog. Scarce a Huet print from which this eager long-eared dog is excluded, but with such conviction is this animal given that the artist must have owned and loved him. So small is each figure of Huet's designs that to find a special object one must hunt over a field of many scattered groups. It is often said of Huet that he seemed to visualize the world in miniature, as through the wrong end of an opera glass.

The wave of classic revival which dominated art after the Revolution and during Napoleon's ascendency gave his pen new motives. As readily as he had drawn gay country fêtes and had scattered little floating islands over the open spaces, just as joyously now he recreated gods and symbols, medallions and geometric lozenges, yet contrived to banish cold formality by the animation of human figures and animals.

Huet came to the Jouy print factory in 1783 and was made its art director. He was with the factory through its richest period, through the difficult days after the Revolution and during the rise of the Empire. He died in 1811 which was not long before the great print works finished their mission in the world. France so values the work of this talented decorative painter, the work that he executed for the Jouy factory, that a collection of his cartoons is preserved in Paris, in the Musée de L'Union Central des Arts Decoratifs.

The print factory at Jouy was so much more important than others that we take its history as an elucidation of the entire industry in Europe. Other factories in France for printing cotton and linen were at Angers, Avignon, Bordeaux, Marseilles, Lyons, etc. They too suffered from the edicts of prohibition and rejoiced in the recalling of all restrictions. They too imported all their cotton calico from the East, when none was made in Europe, and afterwards imported only the cotton wool for their own machines which were constantly improving. And all came to prosperity through the invention of cylinder printing. In the end, that is before 1830, all submitted to a decadence forced by the times.

America's contribution to early textile printing has more value in the world of patriotic sentiment than in the world of the applied arts. For those who are keen to learn of our early endeavors there is much gratifying material and a few textiles in the nature of "documents." Our paucity of examples is of course due to non-production, and that had origin in the early restrictions of England concerning her colonists. Wishing to retain her transplanted people as consumers, she declared through Lord Sheffield that the colonists of North America had no right to manufacture, not even a nail nor a horseshoe.

TOILE DE JOUY, 1800, MONOCHROME. MARRIAGE OF
FIGARO

TOILE DE JOUY, 1804, SIMILAR IN DESIGN TO HUET'S LATER WORK

We have not touched on the printing of silk, nor on archeology. They seem to be wide apart, but recent explorations of archeologists in Chinese Turkestan have revealed bits of printed silk made in an early century, possibly the Eighth. Silk printing had no such vogue as cotton printing in the great century of the industry. It is the modern product of the perfected machine in constant and daily use, and although we are affected by its beauty it tells us no story other than that of present-day prosperity and quick production.

We can take toiles de Jouy as the aristocrats among printed cottons and linens, their artists being the most talented, their factory being the most productive of *bon teint,* as honestly dyed goods were called. Yet in comparison with the print industry of today all the factories of Europe in the Eighteenth Century must seem like small producers.

Jouy fell into decadence through the loss of Oberkampf and of the artist Huet. But printed cloths for decoration could not be suppressed. Today we have them not as a sudden fashion as in the Eighteenth Century but as a steady friend. They are proof against fickle fashion which suddenly rejects what she has

259

passionately loved, because we draw upon such a talented past for historic designs and tints, and have at the same time a fountain ever flowing of new ornament and color.

The place of chintz and cretonne is a definite one nowadays. It is the pleasantest material for the country house of summer use, it is the gayest for bedrooms in either winter or summer, town or country, for in the wide range of quality, design and color almost any furniture can be suited—in curtaining at least.

Chairs and sofas are not entirely satisfactory when covered with cretonne tightly stretched and treated like other upholstery material. The original manner is far more eloquent, the removable cover, preferably with flounces for cushioned pieces. There is about this an informality appropriate to the stuff and suggestive of the time when all the world were making their houses gay and informal.

Climate regulates largely the present use of cretonnes. When weather is hot we long for them. The ideal for the home-lover is a set of chintz or cretonne covers for all seats and couches, which are slipped on in late spring, and which make of the home a new and more charming place. In England where the climate is made of fog and mist for many a winter day, the inclination is to use the bright slip-covers all through the round year, in summer to keep pace with nature, in winter to induce gaiety. Perhaps a pleasure added is the memory of the Georgian times, when Dolly Varden tripped about in her gown of chintz, when Dorothy Vernon wore hers with aristocratic elegance, when the gay ladies of Bath were as beflowered as were the drapings of their houses.

Words seem at times to need a definition, even though they be often on the tongue. Chintz is a word that has a special meaning in England which is not meant here. There it designates a printed cotton which is finished with a stiff glaze by a process of calendering. Here it is used interchangeably with cretonne.

The origin of chintz is a Hindu word which signified colored or flowered—chint. In the time of Samuel Pepys it was so spelled ("bought a chint for my wife"), and only later was an s added which time changed to z.

CHAPTER XVII

DRAPING OF WINDOWS AND BEDS

EVEN as recently as the times of the great Renaissance the window was shamelessly free of draperies. Incredible masses of velvet brocades in designs of magnificence, and damasks and brocatelles in rich hues, were draped wherever draping was possible—except at windows. So we have largely to imagine the method appropriate to our recent Renaissance architecture.

The Renaissance maiden in her jeweled velvet gown peeped out into street or garden from a casement far smaller than the window now. Houses had scarce finished being refuges from an attacking enemy, besides which glass was rare and costly. Glass-makers had not yet arrived at the production of plate-glass, but gave their customers panes that were thick and bubbly, or of the kind called bull's-eye. What need for curtains when even the most inquisitive peeping neighbor could not see through, and the sun itself thrust in a ray with difficulty?

With the Seventeenth Century came larger windows, for then the château was replacing the castle; the noble was changing from a soldier to a courtier. And these large windows developed a style of curtaining. Contrast the old buildings of the Louvre (demolished) with which Francis I was pleased, with the Pavilion Louis XIV in that same palace, to appreciate the change in window size.

The silks of Lyons and of Spitalfields were taking the place of the more Oriental silks of Lucca, Florence and Venice. These were used lavishly on walls, and what more natural than to trail them over onto the wide spaces of the new large windows. Late in the Seventeenth Century the draperies hung in lavish fulness on either side the window, and were finished at the top with a lambrequin very much in the style of the state bed.

When importations began from India, light muslins were among the wares. It is hard to think of a world without cotton textiles, yet until that time Europe had practically none. They arrived opportunely for the increasingly large windows, these transparent muslins. The fashion was to hang one very wide curtain across the entire window with the silken stuff on either side. This single curtain was drawn to one side when occasion required free passage of view or air. And this prevailed until some bright person thought to split in two this muslin veil and make the curtain as we know it now.

With France setting the fashion for more than a hundred years of decorative beauty, we look to the draperies of "the three Louis'" for counsel as to the arranging of our own. In all cases the long curtains were perforce the same in manner, but the difference in style shows mainly in the materials used and in the arrangement across the top which hid the mechanism of the hanging and connected the two lines of curtain drapery.

In the fashion of Louis XIV, the formal lambrequin was used, either plain or cut in dentils or tabs which were trimmed with galloon. The style of Louis XV departed from formality and aimed at a careless richness which seemed to flout the conventions even as did the Court. The lambrequin was replaced by loops and drapings, and these were ornamented with fringe and lace. And last the style of Louis XVI readopted the classic, and became restrained by lessening the amount of material used and employing silks of greater lightness such as taffeta. Lambrequins were arranged in small festoons but of perfect balance; that is, they were alike on both sides of the center. Very narrow tasseled fringe edged these lambrequins.

The fashion for windows in England was practically the same as in France. Indeed all Europe imitated France, or at least attached their own imaginings to the French designs, thus giving the difference peculiar to each country.

Chintzes or cretonnes belonging to this time, made ideal window-dressings. Great as was the craze for them in France, English styles are more faithful to them, for their use has never been discontinued. So accustomed are we to cretonnes that it is hard to think of a world without them, especially in summer when all the house seems dressed en gala with the slip-covers that enliven it.

The lambrequin is made a necessity by the architect who groups three or four windows together. Long curtains cannot hang between each, but only at the end windows. The expanse of sash curtains coming between needs some link between these widely separated breadths, and it is the pleasure of the lambrequins to form that link and thus bring unity to the draping.

Two forms are most suitable in these days when the severity of the modern mode has a restraining effect even on the styles of the Eighteenth Century. The first is the simple straight band with noticeable absence of trimming; the other is cut in an almost architectural arrangement of arches, one over each window of the group, and is deep enough to force attention. The straight curtains at the ends count as columns to sustain this arch, or the lambrequin may descend low at the two outside borders.

It is always the window that decides the manner of its dressing. The arched top high in the room needs at least a shallow draping or a lambrequin that follows those same shallow lines, unless the long heavy curtain is skilfully draped to form a protection from the high light during the day. It is this individuality of the window that makes the curtaining of the house a problem.

When France was setting the fashions at Versailles and in the numberless houses of La Pompadour, du Barry and the imitating courtiers, the mode required

266

AMERICAN HOME-WOVEN BEDCOVERS OF EARLY NINETEENTH CENTURY
WOVEN ON NARROW LOOMS AND SEAMED. PATRIOTIC EMBLEMS FORM
THE DESIGNS

Metropolitan Museum of Art

LOUIS XVI BEDROOM WHICH MIGHT BE HAPPILY COPIED TODAY

many tasseled fringes, much figured galloon worked in scrolls. Today we are forced to eliminate many elaborate details even while adopting the spirit of a style, for it is an age in which we must reckon with the smoke and dust of motor-cars, and industrialism, and in towns, of the huge heated apartment-houses.

The desire to let light into the room, especially in towns, has made a difference in the type of window drapings. Thin fabrics are preferred to thick, and linings are often banished as in the case of taffeta. That marvelous material called rayon so well imitates the silk-worm's thread that taffeta and gauze are possible to all. Modernistic decorators make free use of these in getting severe effects which are pleasingly simple. A group of windows, for example, is hung with voile in three shades of one color, laid one over the other. A full curtain to the floor is of the lightest shade; a second curtain over that falls two thirds of the way, and a third curtain, the darkest, falls but one third of the way. Thus the window is a flood of transparent color deepening towards the heavens.

A large-meshed silk net in silver color is used by the modernists to screen the sash or to border an alcove in a full mass almost like the waterfall of a summer brook. Pompeian red, cobalt blue, or jade green are similarly used except that the window panes are left clear and a valance stretches across the top to connect the fluffy curtains, and this valance is made of layer on layer, opulently full like a ballet skirt. The effect is as gay and amusing as the presence of a *première danseuse*.

Sash curtains of printed voile laid nearly flat and without division in the center of the window look like a new sort of painted glass, but as different from old stained-glass windows as the modern window-pane is from the leaded one.

With the inclination to preserve light rather than to block it out, the sash curtain takes on such importance as to make possible the banishment of the heavy hanging. Among the modern fabrics are voiles and nets, which carry a pattern in white floss, sketchy but effective. The lightest of these when seen against the pane seem like an etching on the glass. More striking are the heavier modernistic drawing of palm leaves, and even a vision of horizontal clouds with a setting sun behind them—all in white or cream, of course.

Is it freakish to use odd materials for heavy draperies at the window? Perhaps, but with magic in his hands, the modern eccentric can employ with good effect such things as suède leather, black patent cloth (which looks like lacquer) and silvered leather, which hangs with severity yet with soft radiance and if it has a tape-wide border of jade or some bright hue, it is an entrancing addition to a reception-room of today.

The fairies seem to work on looms that produce a white voile covered with large modernistic design brocaded in white velvet. With light filtering through, the value of voile is lost and the strange velvet motive floats like a chain of soft white figures against the day.

As exclusive patterns peculiar to the occupant of the house are a desideratum in the home of modern decoration, the pattern of the curtain may be designed by him who designed the room, and translated into satin appliqué on voile.

THE REVERENCED BED

The tendency of our day is to suppress the bed, to make of it a couch with the footboard abolished, or to obliterate its true character under innumerable silken cushions. To understand the pompous magnificence of the bed of earlier centuries one must realize the place it occupied in social—and even political—life, and it at once gains importance as an expression of other times and other manners.

Baldaquins, canopies, testers, all tell a tale, and curtains speak of display as well as comfort. In the time of Francis I it was a courtesy for a gentleman to put his bed at the service of a guest, actually to take him in as a bed-fellow. It must have been a severe strain on courtesy to take a formal sleep beside a snoring prince or nightmarish noble. Yet one hears that Francis I thus favored Charles IX, and the Duc de Guise the great Condé. Other customs there were equally demanding and all of them together give reason for the draperies which we use today in bedrooms of sufficient size. Oddly enough the principal bed in the house served as a reception room. While still between the sheets of slumber's hours the man or woman of importance admitted persons who came on business or on friendship's quest. Silk-covered extra pillows were provided for the recliner to place beneath

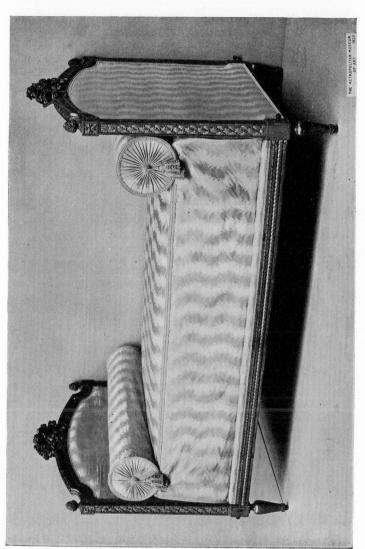

LOUIS XVI BED WITH TAUT DRAPING

BED À LA DUCHESSE, HANGINGS AND COVERLET OF
TAPESTRY STYLE LOUIS XVI

the elbow, that guests might be greeted or papers signed with greater ease.

It was etiquette in the time of Louis XIV and earlier thus to receive visits of State. But most amusing was the custom prevailing among women of higher rank. On the loss of her husband the widow spent three weeks in bed in order to receive in appropriate setting the ensuing visits of condolence.

Catherine de' Medici, always interesting and intriguing because of the times she reflected, presents a magnificent picture of the luxury of woe. On the death of Henri II she tore down the gorgeous brocades of the bed and replaced them with more of magnificence than even color could express. Into this bed they popped the widowed queen, and this is how it was draped. A canopy was over her head of black silk damask lined with white. From this depended a dossier which hung behind the bed's head, also of black damask, but embroidered in silver. But the fine effect was given by the curtains long and full, all of black velvet. They were embroidered with gold and silver and finished across the hem with silver fringe. When they parted it was to reveal the queen lying under a coverlid of black velvet and black damask set off with flashes of silver and pearls. Who could doubt the sincerity of woe thus beautifully expressed? This style of bed was aptly called the *lit de parade*.

Yet again, Francis I the elegant and artistic father-in-law of Catherine when wishing to curry favor with Henry VIII of England took with him a gift of a "camp-bed" in crimson velvet lavishly embroidered with fruit worked in real pearls.

The flight of Mary of Scots to England is one of the historic events which always stirs us. She was widowed, beautiful, and, oh, so young for the part she played. But she took with her thirty beds to soften the bleakness of her Scottish castle. Velvet ones were in the mossy green of summer woods, and they were also draped in crimson and in brown. There were damask ones as well, and satin, and these displayed shades of red, of blue, of yellow, and some were of white made lovelier by gold embroidery. All of them were rich with trimmings of metal and of silk.

It would appear that great ladies changed the hangings of the bed as capriciously or as reasonably as they changed their gowns. We are told that they were sometimes short of stockings, especially those of silk, but never short of drapings for the vanities of the bed-chamber. Thus it came that the decorator and upholsterer grew ever more important, and the skilled sculptor in wood was without a bed to carve. Beds were so concealed by draperies that it was no longer reasonable to spend time and money carving them as they were carved in the days of Italy's High Renaissance.

Later the large square canopy disappeared and with it the long curtains shrunk to a drapery over the bed's head.

It was not altogether because of the cold that beds were curtained; it was to give dignity and prominence to the most important piece of furniture in the house. It is the habit of today to speak with flippancy of all things, a charming and witty flippancy. Nevertheless we can appreciate the sentiment of older times. I find it hard to express in modern phrase the respect with which the bed was regarded when it was considered worthy of such elegant caparison as we have been considering. Generations of deep sentiment about birth and marriage and death had crystallized into reverence.

Thus it was the bed as a family altar, or as a king's subsidiary throne, that it was considered appropriate to dress with ultra magnificence, this dress to be changed for varying circumstance.

And when now we drape our beds after the olden manner, a haunting seriousness flits through the back of the mind.

AMERICAN BED COVERS

Notwithstanding the claims of long descent of the typical New England Vere de Vere, most of the early colonists were simple people with the resources of the class that makes the backbone of the nation. In spite of England's prohibiting the manufacture of even a nail the art of weaving began at an early date.

But it was a cottage art. No housemother is willing to see her family shiver in the severities of winter. So looms were built that occupied the corner of the kitchen, and spinning-wheels became as common then as the radio now, as an adjunct to family life in its hours of relaxation.

As yarn of a natural color becomes monotonous in a textile, the able woman of the colonies wandered in woods and fields for dyes, plants that would yield color for the dye-pot. Thus indigo was found, that valuable vegetable growth for which commercial England was ever seeking in her colonies.

Instead of tracing the advance of weaving in America, from the cottage industry to its place in the present overpowering industrialism, it is more interesting to confine a brief word to that fine example of home work, the figured bed-spread or coverlet. Usually it is of dark blue and white, wool and cotton, and those who possess examples of this evidence of home art are ever glowing with an inward content.

These relics make a mind picture because of the circumstances under which they were woven, and because of the *zeit-geist* they represent. They were the fancy-work of the late Eighteenth and early Nineteenth Centuries, occupying all the hours that might have been a woman's hours of leisure. But, the loom in order, and the warp threads spun and strung in place, the work impelled. Once the woof of soft wool began to record itself in an inch or two of finished fabric, it teased the weaver to continue, to set for herself a daily ambition of inches. And so the cloth grew amid the daily round of duties and complexities of family life.

The wool was home raised as a matter of course. The yarn was home spun. The dyeing was an affair of indoors and out, of finding first the needed plants, of long conferences with neighbors as to best methods of treating these; then of dipping and of that important element of permanence in color, the mordant.

The pattern itself began with a simple variance of the geometric, squares in blue, in mixed blue and white, of varying sizes all forming a larger square. Other colors besides blue were sought, and so soft reds and wood tones replaced the blue. Later came scarlet and the brilliant green, but with them a loss of the restraint that constitutes charm.

Numberless are the weaves on the lines of squares or plaids, all softened by the tricks of the ambitious weaver, yet scarcely varying from the geometric. Gradually the art grew more sophisticated, and rounded motives were introduced as well as leaf shapes, still retaining the general effect of lines of squares on the whole field of the quilt.

As the art advanced a border was invented as a finish. The bed of those days was a high four-poster with a feather bed in place of hair mattress, a white petticoat valance below. This seemed to demand a finish more important than the selvedge, and so it came, timidly at first and then divertingly. Center and border were in harmony, both carrying some of the same motives. If leaves appeared in the center, trees were on the border. One delicious touch is that each pattern had a name. There is a book on this subject by E. C. Hall wherein one may read pages and pages of these names, which are delightfully imaginative and fantastic. Some of them are romantic, like Lonely Heart, Star of Venus, Lily of the West, and Rosy Walk. Others are historic, like Indian War, Washington's Victory, Mexican Banner and Bonaparte's Retreat.

After the War of the Revolution and after Washington had tied the States together in harmony, the home-woven quilts began to express the political enthusiasm of the men who talked and smoked around the fire while the housewife wove her daily stint.

Then came designs of eagles, their far-spread wings shown in the conventional square, and stars near them told of the emblem of our new-made flag. After the War of 1812 the Capitol with its mounting dome took place of trees for border motive. And both these typical designs introduced lettering in the corners, either patriotic, like, "United we stand, divided we fall," or prophetic, like, "Agriculture and manufacture are the foundation of our independence." It is safe to put these well within the Nineteenth Century.

As the hand loom was never a large affair, the bed covers were woven in two parts and seamed together in the middle, the pattern being executed with regard to this exigency.

Knowing their history it is not strange that we value these old weavings and like them for use as draperies if not for coverlets.

CHAPTER XVIII

MODERNISTIC TEXTILES

JUST before the Great War certain enthusiasts were bringing us textiles from the school of art that had its most productive center in Vienna. Perhaps because it was cheaper for experimentation these fabrics depended on printing for their ornament rather than on weave. They were in the class of cretonne or chintz, and thus within the reach of the modest buyer, or the experimental user.

In their way they were startling. It was as though the "Nude Descending a Stair" had gone from the walls of the first modernist painting exhibition to establish a factory for decorative textiles—and these were the result of her peculiar psyche. Colors were crude, designs were eccentric, unfinished, like a child's work under the kindergartner. Some of us laughed with the pleasure of being tickled with a straw, others were filled with impatience and snorted in anger. But no one could see these new designs applied to their own

279

home furnishings, for they seemed actually to insult the classic modes. More than that, they ignominiously drew much of their composition on the old lines, distorting them yet resembling, and that offense seemed worst of all.

Then certain daring ones took up the Viennese idea of black and white, eschewing entirely the much criticized color schemes, and, thus limited to form and contrast, produced some original and stirring rooms. Silver took the place of white in the best of these, stripes of silver on black velvet, for draperies, silvered walls, black carpets and so on.

The new mode came also from Paris, where young men in revolt against eternal copying were finding joy in experiment and in gleefully upsetting the mannered brushes and pens of the past. We remember Paul Poiret's experiments in color for women's dress. The department of the fine arts felt the same urge and so we saw strange canvases by Cézanne, Matisse, Picasso, Gauguin, but these being out of the province of a book on textiles we respectfully turn from them.

And now today what have we? A well-established department of modernist decorative art with its own list of creators, its own type of patrons. No longer can it be ignored as a passing eccentricity. Moreover it steadily hammers with pretty tappings on the old ideas of taste whether one will or no. Everywhere one turns there are evidences. Shop windows are full of strange trifles, piquant and interesting, which one does not resent. Such an object as a cigarette box cut from solid onyx with no ornament whatever, nor hinge nor handle, depending for beauty on its simple solid form of well-studied proportion, forces one to feel that a box of the old style with metal stand and binding is tawdry in comparison, though both styles are displayed together.

And speaking of shops, it is within their alluring doors one finds some of the best results of modernist effort. The effect is never startling, that special claim for notice being past with decorators of the first rank. The shop window gives evidence of the sort of thing found within, by the style of its curtaining and its background. Some new textile is bound to be used, not startling but expressing tasteful restraint and elegance.

Again the theater has announced itself an upholder of the ever-growing style called modernistic. The drop curtain has for some time been insidiously instilling into our minds the idea that the old type of painted or embroidered "drop" is less suited to our hours of entertainment than one that delicately suggests, that piques the imagination instead of killing it.

Plays of modern life, of old problems oddly solved by hard young persons, smart, unemotional, scientific, such plays are not set among the fluffy curves of the rococo but in the glass, steel, wood and textiles of severe outline with which modern art and life are but complemented. And the most conservative of the beauty-lovers will see beauty here because here is also fitness.

Thus against our will we are awakened to the merit of what we at first resented or visited with our ridicule. There is still much to disapprove. Only a true artist can play with the new toy. It is more exacting than the old, for each problem grows into an education, each room to decorate becomes an adventure.

Textiles for the new manner are a stimulating department of the whole. Those of the time before the war declared themselves too much in their style of ornament and arresting color. Cheapness of manufacture

282

mattered greatly. Therefore printing instead of weaving carried the ornament. Heavy cottons and even jute, or a mixture of the two, distinguished the weave. Linen was rarely used, nor silk except of very light quality.

The situation now has changed. It is the weave which carries the ornament in most important fabrics for decoration of rooms of elegance. Artists of consequence design these textiles, which are patented to prevent their being copied and thrown liberally upon the market. Paul Rodier has composed a design of shaded discs in two or three sizes which he calls "The Mechanical World." At once you see the wheels go 'round, whether of motor-cars or factories, or the disc of a victrola revolves. And this suggestive stuff is woven in but two shades of gray-brown, the magic of the weave suggesting more tones.

Rodier has another textile in the same neutral colors, a design which fills the width from selvedge to selvedge, with undulating wave lines at the bottom on which rides a ship, its full sail tossing among round clouds which fill the heavens.

The former textile is for curtains or for furniture

covering; the other to be hung as a panel on the wall behind a sofa or a bed's head, or wherever the softening effect of decorated wall cloth is needed. Such designs are well used when applied to screens, each width making a panel of distinction, suggesting hand work of some individual kind. These textiles, be it noted, are never self-assertive, even such designs as those just cited. The day for that is past. The present attempt is to induce calm in the room with the once-sought note-of-color effected by a lacquer or highly polished metal like nickel or pewter as a part of a piece of furniture.

Hunt Dietrich with his vivid drawing of animals has inspired many a modernist fabric, as is seen in the attenuated gazelle that is woven as flat as his sheet-iron silhouettes. Robert Chanler's use of fish as decorative motives for painting has been appropriated by a textile mill which gives, by weaving in multicolor, a fish design which is scarce a design, only a suggestion. And this manner of treatment breathes a charm which complete realism would fail to impart and makes the singular subject a pleasant one with which to live.

Raoul Dufy contributes generous leaf designs for

284

silk weaving which retain his characteristics. These and many others are in three-dimensional drawing.

The flat unshaded figure is favored by the stencilers for obvious reasons of technique. Stenciled silks of thin texture, and voiles of cotton, silk or rayon are freely used in dressing windows and for lamp-shades. The manner of making these patterns strongly resembles the toilsome process of the early chintz or cretonne printers in the Seventeenth and Eighteenth Centuries. Clever inventors banished these after years of experiment, and the industrial world felt that a new sun had arisen with the invention of printing from plates and then from cylinders. Now the stencilers of the new mode go back to the hand-block, stamped with painstaking care.

There is in Paris a woman whose silks are much sought. Her method is to sit before a length of white silk and begin to paint on it any outline that occurs to her, discs, blocks, points, half-moons, anything at all that fills the space. One rule she follows that there shall be no background, that all shall be figures or part of figures, also that every imaginable clear color shall be used, but in high key. She keeps herself at the task until something like a harmony of line and color is produced in a space a yard or so in length. Then she hands the silk to her aids who cut stencils and repeat the design after the hand-block and painting process.

Exclusiveness is a high desideratum in such of the new fabrics. This artist's inventions are never duplicated. One length of silk and one only is stenciled or hand-blocked, never to be repeated. To employ this silk in a way to show its beauty and its bewildering design it should be hung against the light. It then has the gay harmony of the bits of glass in a kaleidoscope. Its fields of color although bright are kept too small to dominate, hence there is no clash with other colors in the room. At night the thin silk all covered with design passes for a heavier hanging.

The school at Vienna which produces this silk sends out many others in the new style. Artists from Paris work at these and add their talent and ingenuity of design. But it is noticeable that decorators on this side of the water incline to moderation, and prefer large fields of subdued color to a confusion of tints and sharply defined ornament. Schemes for rooms are

BEDROOM OF EMPRESS JOSEPHINE

Park Avenue Galleries

MODERNISTIC DINING-ROOM IN SILVER GRAY BLACK AND ORANGE

composed with the admirable intent of conferring calm upon the occupant, calm and quiet being rarities in modern life. A room typical has a floor of jade-green lac on which is thrown a rug of black lightly broken with an eccentric line of gray, walls and ceiling are silvered, curtains are of chartreuse gauze, and lighting flows from shafts of frosted glass, applied to corners. When the problem comes of a covering for furniture, recourse must be had to the woven patterns in rayon and cotton where the rayon threads carry the design against a grayish ground and shine like silver to carry on the effect of the walls.

Furniture itself being pronounced and striking, bibelots the same, all forms, in fact, being in startling contrast to those with which we are familiar, the inclination is to keep all upholstered furniture low in tone, avoiding sharp design. Curtains and wall hangings however give abundant welcome to the figured textiles. To meet the need for solid colors and meet it with intelligence and originality we find special textiles resembling the old but with the peculiar difference that marks the modernistic.

Pile fabrics such as velvets are not the suave, even

weave of the ages, but take on the roughened look of fustian, low in gloss and sometimes with the warp threads showing in contrasting color. Other long-piled velvets, glossier than these, are crushed to give variety by breaking up the fields of light and shadow that characterize the velvet proper. Plain old satins are not disdained as seats and cushions in chairs where all else is covered with a damask.

The new treatment of walls calls for new style textiles to hang upon them—not in full curtaining as of old, for such a manner would be too soft, too reminiscent of sentiment and emotion, but in panels of decoration. Fancy a room lined with a light wood in the natural color as it glows under a finish of wax, marked off into panels by bands of steel or nickel combined with black; or fancy a room whose walls are covered with twenty-inch stripes of cork in three shades, or one whose walls are covered with silver leaf or pale gilt roughly applied, and you can see the need of some softener like a textile panel. Our human bodies are made of such tender stuff, so easily bruised, that the instinct favors some soft refuge—even though it be only for the vision to rest upon.

And so come the modernistic panels to supply a milder decoration than glass or metal. We have already noted the effects of Rodier in this direction. Dufy's brocade designs are sufficiently decorative and large in scale to serve. But the most characteristic are the hangings made as a painting is made, through the creative genius of an artist. Foremost among these, leaving out painting, are the tapestries.

But except for the old tapestry technique in the weave, the cartoons resemble not at all the tapestry with which we are familiar—with the single exception of a large-warped, rough hanging reminiscent of the poorer specimens from ancient Peru.

As the eye sees first the picture in a tapestry and as the weave is similar in all, it is in the cartoon that the modern differs from the masters of the past. Here one finds the new school of drawing in the joy of unconvention. Maximilian Wenceslaus of the Viennese school dares human figures of strange new movement, and Jean Luçat of Paris indicates in two square yards of slight detail the salient points of all Algeria, Atlas Mountains, blue sea and cruel desert with amazing vegetation.

Needless to say, these tapestries, whether of geometric design or more thoughtful drawing, are not executed with the old-time beauty of weave. Indeed the lover of old Arras and Brussels work would hesitate to call them tapestries at all. But it is doubtless felt that the coarseness of the weave and the roughness of the wool in modern work gives an informality of texture appropriate to modern decoration. At least it defies the old convention in still one more department of textiles.

The use of pictures having grown rarer and rarer on walls of all but galleries, the textile is intended to take their place. They are hung wherever the wall looks barest, but always in harmony with the architecture of the room. Modern mantels having lost their shelves, and consequently their row of ornaments, the textile panel is happily displayed upon the chimney breast. It hangs above the sofa and adds to the coziness of that friendly piece of furniture, and hangs behind the head-board of a bed. Apropos, it makes a most attractive coverlet, especially for the couch bed which is sure to be found in some room of an apartment.

Screens are so often painted, so often silvered or gilded with a gay little motive to break the large field,

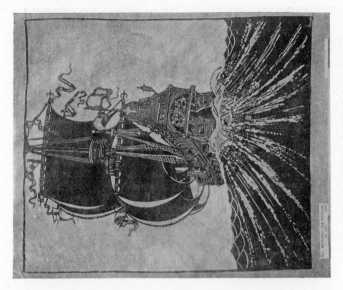

LINOLEUM BLOCK PRINT ON LINEN

AMERICAN PRINTED SILK OF TODAY

Park Avenue Galleries

SITTING-ROOM IN MODERNIST STYLE, WALLS COVERED RAYON IN LIGHT WOOD TONES, CORRUGATED CEILING IN SIMILAR SHADES. THE FURNITURE COVERINGS REPEAT THE BROWNISH TONES, LAMPSHADES ARE OF BROWN LEATHER AND THE CARPET IS PLAIN GREEN

that few are left for textiles to cover. But should the softer effect be desired the woven panel comes in play, the stencil supplemented with the brush, and here may be used many of the large designs that only repeat themselves once in every yard. Many of the rayon fabrics are used for curtains, heavy stuffs in golden beige or warm taupe which carry the design in weaving only. The gloss of this wonder-thread makes its own variations of light and shade.

It might be said of modernistic prints that those most easily used are timid in color though not in design. The high key is preferred where many colors are introduced, and thus all blend easily with each other and with the various objects in the room. Others avoid all colors save shades of beige, gray and the various neutrals that waver between the two, warm with a reddish cast or olive with slight green.

When an exception is made and the figures stand out boldly, the print is used more for cushions than for entire sets of furniture. A sofa of crushed velvet in gray is interestingly enlivened with a big cushion of orange figures well covering a ground of black.

The new printed textiles are dangerous playthings

for the amateur. They are not the simple toys they look. Each one has an individuality most self-assertive. It has moreover a captious quarrelsome nature that relishes disagreement with its neighbor. These traits are not revealed until the amateur has the hangings in the home. They are not composed at hazard; each one is the result of concentrated thought and of thorough sympathy with the spirit of the new decoration; and only the professional has the instinct for style that directs a harmonious arrangement.

We have spoken of stenciled heavy fabrics. These are made exclusively for the especial place they occupy. Often they carry arresting motives and colors, but as they are used only as panels or screens their presence is but discreetly stimulating.

The matter of ornament has occupied most of the pages of this book, not so much its forms as the history of other times which has crystallized into these particular compositions. Race growth, social customs, religious worship and development, all are composed into designs which have been used throughout the ages. What of these strange unreadable mixtures that are given us as today's expression and which we are expected to substitute for the old? They are said to express the spirit of our times. I wonder if they do, or if they do not express only the hasty sequence of novelty which arises from youth's constant demand. This remark, please note, applies not to the movement as a whole but to its ornament alone.

Continuing with prints lest the more alluring be left out, there is offered us wide choice of beauty in printed voiles, chiffon, *mousseline de soie,* and other gauzy fabrics. Their obvious use is curtains or lamp-shades where the light filters through and makes all color diaphanous. New schemes of lighting aim at the indirect ray. A room, they say, should be as full of light as is a fishbowl and with no more evidence of its source. All persons over twenty-five hail the indirect lighting with enthusiasm because it casts no shadows on a tired face, and the methods of introducing it are curiously beautiful.

But there still remain those who like the luminous refuge of a shaded lamp especially accompanied by a book, and therefore the new style leaves us this ancient household god. Here in the lamp's shade is found use for new patterns in printed silk and gauzes. The finely pleated shade is gone, the shapes have altered, all trimmings are absent, but the new designs and plain transparent weaves without design make a more than happy change.

Unflattering it is to our vanity, but we must confess that the most beautiful and interesting of all new decorative printed textiles are those composed in Europe, with especial emphasis on Paris and Vienna. But this condition will not forever prevail. Our designers are becoming aware that science and an inexorable principle of strength and even of mathematics underlies the new movement, and according to this they create. And as for ornament that deals with figures, human and animal, the artist who designs best for the style modernistic is he who is longest steeped in the ancient.

A FINAL WORD

As the object of this book is to add to the interest in decoration through its textiles, an exhaustive description of technique is not attempted, but merely a few words of elucidation. The following books which have been consulted by the author are suggested as reading for those who wish to pursue the study with greater seriousness.

LES SOIRERIES D'ART. Raymond Cox.

ORNAMENT IN EUROPEAN SILK. Alan S. Cole.

RECEUIL DES DESSINS. E. Dumonthier.

L'ART MUSSULMAN. Gaston Migeon.

ORNAMENT OF TEXTILE FABRICS. F. Fishback.

DECORATIVE SILKS. Otto von Falke.

PARACAS (Peruvian). Jean Levillier.

ORIENTAL ART. R. Koechlin and G. Migeon.

L'ART DE LA PERSE ANCIENNE. G. Crès.

PAINTED AND PRINTED FABRICS. Henri Clouzot. With American section by Frances Morris.

HISTORY OF TAPESTRY. Eugene Müntz.

INDEX

171-

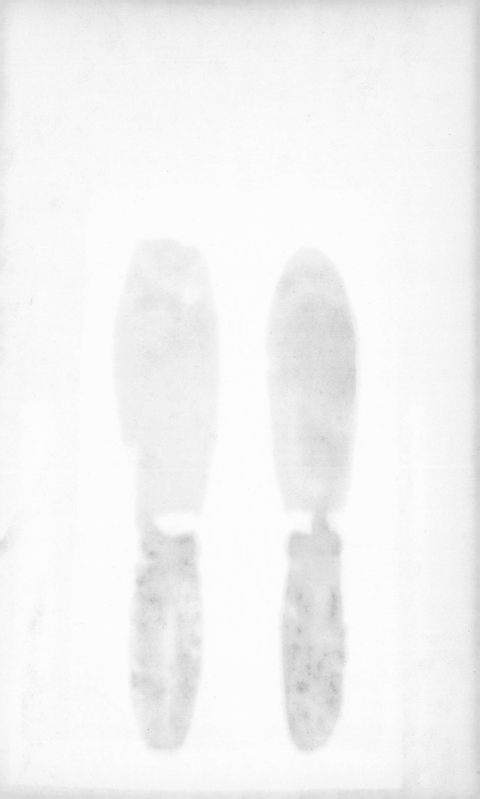